Leyland Cars—Sales

Leyland Cars—Service

© BRITISH LEYLAND UK LIMITED 1976

Driver's Handbook
TOURER (GHN 5)
and GT (GHD 5)

Publication Part No. AKM 3661

FOREWORD

This Handbook introduces you to your Leyland car. Your car is built to a high standard of quality and reliability and with good driving, correct car care and regular maintenance should give you carefree and economical motoring.

The introductory pages cover the operation and function of the controls, switches and general equipment fitted.

The main part of the Handbook gives detailed information on jacking, wheel changing, bulb renewal, lubrication and the servicing procedure of components.

Regular maintenance at the recommended intervals is essential to maintain your car at the original standard of efficiency and you will find our detailed recommendations under **'MAINTENANCE SUMMARY'**. Those items which require specialized equipment should be carried out by a Distributor or Dealer. Refer to the **'GENERAL DATA'** for information required during servicing and the day-to-day running of the vehicle such as tyre pressures, oil capacities, etc.

Our Distributors and Dealers are trained and available to service your car for you, and details of our maintenance scheme are included in your **Passport to Service**. Look for the **Leycare** sign.

References to right- or left-hand are made as if the car is being viewed from the rear.

CONTENTS

INTRODUCTION TO THE CAR

Page
- CONTROLS .. 4
- INSTRUMENTS AND SWITCHES .. 5
- STARTING AND RUNNING INSTRUCTIONS .. 12
- LOCKS, FITTINGS AND BODY .. 16
- SEATS AND SEAT BELTS .. 27
- HEATING AND VENTILATING .. 30

CARE OF THE CAR

- CLEANING .. 32
- COOLING SYSTEM .. 33
- WHEELS AND TYRES .. 36
- BRAKES AND MASTER CYLINDERS .. 39
- ELECTRICAL .. 43
- IGNITION .. 54
- ENGINE .. 56
- FUEL SYSTEM .. 59
- TRANSMISSION .. 61
- STEERING/SUSPENSION .. 63
- GENERAL DATA .. 64
- LEYLAND ST .. 67
- MAINTENANCE SUMMARY .. 68
- SERVICE .. 72
- LUBRICATION .. 75

CONTROLS

Fig. 1
Gear lever (1) The gear positions are indicated on the lever knob. To engage reverse gear move the lever to the left in the neutral position until resistance is felt, apply further side pressure to overcome the resistance and then pull the lever back to engage the gear. The reverse lights operate automatically when reverse is selected with the ignition switched on.

Synchromesh engagement is provided on all forward gears.

Overdrive switch (2) A slide switch incorporated in the gear lever knob operates the overdrive. To engage the overdrive move the switch rearward; to disengage, move the switch forward. For operating instructions see page 14.

Hand brake (3) The hand brake is of the pull-up lever type, operating mechanically on the rear wheels only. To release the hand brake pull the lever up slightly, depress the button on the end of the lever and push the lever down.

Pedals (4) (5) (6) The pedals are arranged in the conventional positions.

The brake pedal operates the brake hydraulic system and applies the brakes on all four wheels, also bringing the stop warning lights into operation when the ignition is switched on.

Mixture control (Choke) (7) To enrich the fuel air mixture and assist starting when the engine is cold, pull out the knob and turn a quarter of a turn clockwise to lock the control in the position selected. To release the control turn it in an anti-clockwise direction and push it inwards.

DO NOT MOVE the control in or out whilst it is in the locked position. Notes on setting the control are given on page 13.

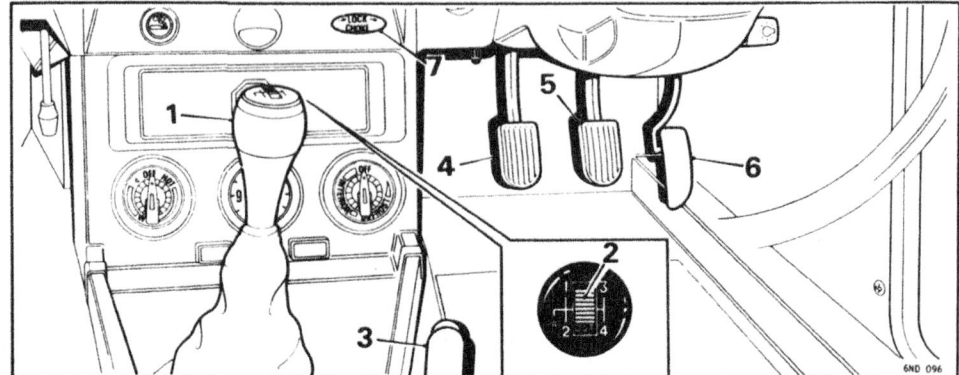

Fig. 1

INSTRUMENTS AND SWITCHES

IGNITION/STARTER SWITCH AND STEERING LOCK *Fig. 1*

Key number The key number appears on the key, on the number tag supplied or on a label attached to the windscreen of a new car.

NOTE THE KEY NUMBER in your **DIARY** and in a reference book at **HOME** and then **REMOVE THE LABEL** with the key number **FROM THE CAR**. Consult your Distributor/Dealer regarding key replacements for the steering-column lock.

The steering-column lock (4), if used properly, will greatly reduce the possibility of the car being stolen.

Unlocking To unlock the steering, insert the key and turn it to position 'I'. If the steering-wheel has been turned to engage the lock, slight movement of the steering-wheel will assist disengagement of the lock plunger.

With the key in the position marked 'I' the ignition is switched off and the steering lock disengaged. The radio may be operated with the key in this position. The key must be in this position when towing the car for recovery.

Ignition and start To switch on the ignition, turn the key to position 'II'. Further movement against spring resistance to position 'III' operates the starter motor. Release the key immediately the engine starts.

Locking To lock the steering, turn the key anti-clockwise to the position marked 'I', press the button (5), turn the key to the 'O' position and withdraw it.

WARNING. The steering lock/ignition/starter switch and its electrical circuits are designed to prevent the ignition system and starter from being energized while the steering lock is engaged. Serious consequences could result from alterations or substitution of the steering lock/ignition switch or its wiring. In no circumstances must the ignition switch be separated from the steering lock.

Do not lubricate the steering lock.

Fig. 1

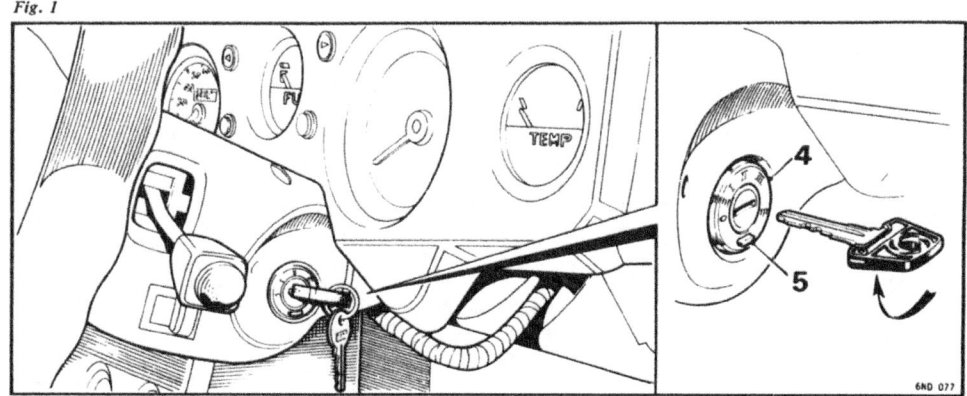

Instruments and Switches

INSTRUMENTS *Fig. 2*

Speedometer (1)   In addition to indicating the road speed this instrument also records the total distance (3) and the distance travelled for any particular trip (2). To reset the trip recorder, turn the knob (4) anti-clockwise; it is important that all the counters are returned to zero.

Tachometer (5)   This instrument indicates the revolutions per minute of the engine and assists the driver to use the most effective engine speed range for maximum performance in any gear (see page 14).

Oil pressure gauge (6)   The gauge registers the pressure of the oil in the engine lubricating system. Important notes on its indications are given on page 13.

Coolant temperature gauge (7)   The gauge indicates the temperature of the coolant as it leaves the engine cylinder head. An important note about temperature is given on page 14.

Fuel gauge (8)   When the ignition is switched on the fuel gauge indicates approximately the amount of fuel in the tank. An important note on filling with fuel is given on page 12.

Clock (9)   To start the clock or reset the hands, press and turn the button until the hands are at the correct time; pull the button lightly to ensure the reset has disengaged.

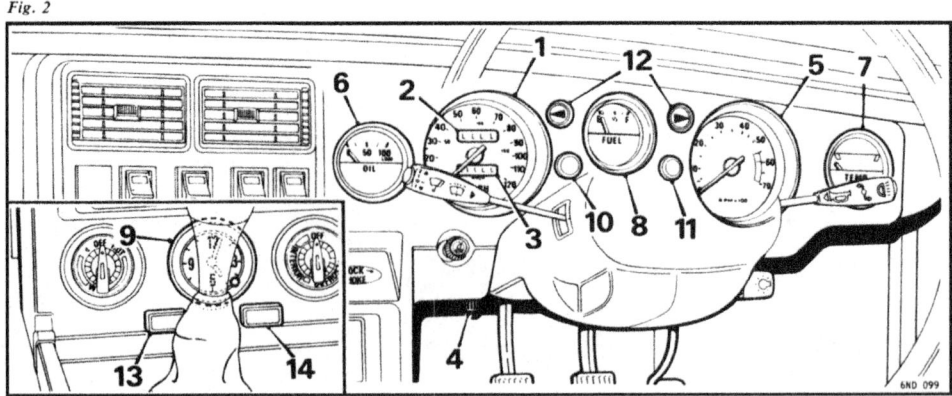

Fig. 2

WARNING LIGHTS *Fig. 2*

Ignition (10)   RED. This light serves the dual purpose of reminding the driver to switch off the ignition and of being a no-charge indicator.

Main beam (11)   BLUE. The light glows when the headlights are switched on with the beams in the raised position. The light goes out when the beams are dipped.

Direction indicator (12)   GREEN. The warning light flashes when the direction indicators are operating. Additional warning is also given by the audible 'clicking' of the flasher unit.

Hazard (12)   GREEN. The direction indicator warning lights will flash when the hazard warning lights are operating.

Hand brake (13)   RED. The warning light glows when the hand brake is applied and the ignition is switched on.

> NOTE: As an automatic check the 'BRAKE' warning lamp will glow each time the ignition key is turned to position **'III'** (starter motor operating). Consult your Distributor or Dealer if the 'BRAKE' warning lamp fails to glow when the starter is operated.

Seat belt (14)   RED. The warning light will glow when the ignition is switched on if the driver's seat belt is not fastened.

Instruments and Switches

SWITCHES *Fig. 3*

Lighting (1)   Press the switch lever downwards to the central position to switch on the side and tail lamps, and fully down for the headlights.

Panel lamps (2)   The panel lights will function only when the side lamps are switched on. Turning the switch knob clockwise switches on the panel lights; further clockwise movement of the knob reduces the light brilliance.

Heated rear window (GT) (if fitted) (3)   The heated rear window will operate only when the ignition is switched on. The green illumination light on the face of the switch glows when the panel lights are switched on. Notes on the use of the heated rear window can be found under **'LOCKS, FITTINGS AND BODY'**.

Courtesy light (4)   The courtesy light is controlled by a switch on the fascia and by a switch fitted to each door pillar. With the doors closed the light may be switched on by pressing the lower end of the switch rocker. Opening either door will switch on the light and closing the door will extinguish the light. The green illumination light on the face of the switch glows when the panel lights are switched on.

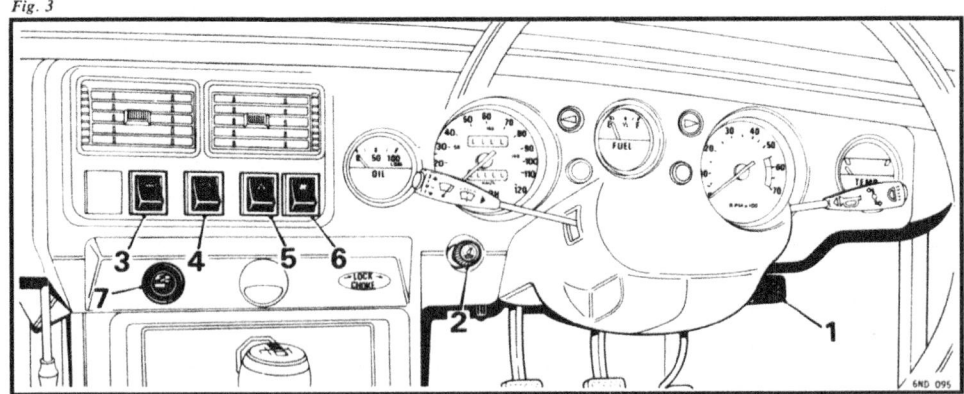

Fig. 3

Hazard warning To use the direction indicators as a hazard warning to other road users, press the lower end of the switch rocker: all the direction indicators and their warning lights will operate together, irrespective of whether the ignition is on or off. The green illumination light on the face of the switch glows when the panel lights are switched on.

Return the switch to the off position to cancel the hazard warning.

Blower switch and heater controls (6) For operating instructions see **'HEATING AND VENTILATING'**.

Cigar-lighter (7) To operate, press the knob inwards and release. When the element has become sufficiently heated the lighter will be partially ejected, and may then be withdrawn for use. The rim of the cigar-lighter is illuminated when the panel lights are switched on.

Instruments and Switches

COLUMN SWITCH *Fig. 4*

Windscreen Washer and Wiper Control (1)

Windscreen washer Press the end of the lever inwards ('**A**') to operate the washer jets.

The washer reservoir should be filled with a mixture of water and **UNIPART Screenwash**. In freezing conditions use **UNIPART 'Four Seasons' Screenwash**. To avoid possible damage to paintwork **do not** use radiator anti-freeze in the windscreen washer.

Windscreen wiper Move the lever downwards ('**B**') and then release it to obtain a single wipe. The lever will return to the 'off' position and the blades will park automatically at the completion of the wipe.

To operate the wipers at normal speed move the lever up to the first position ('**C**') and to the second position ('**D**') when a higher wiping speed is required.

NOTE: Neither the windscreen wiper nor the washer can operate until the ignition has been switched on.

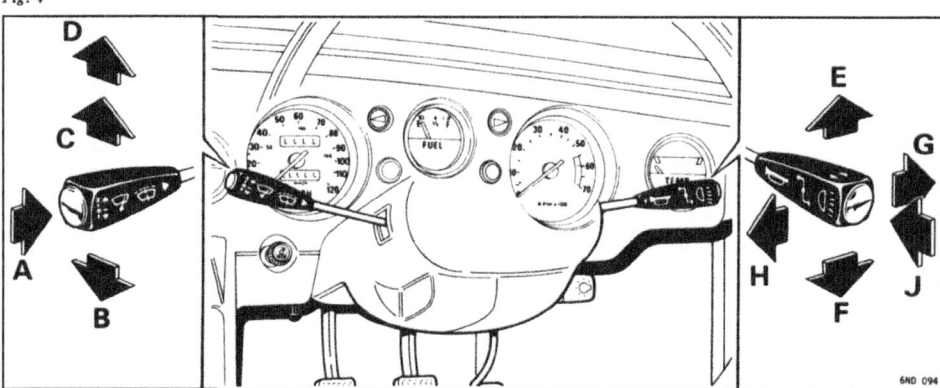

Fig. 4

Direction Indicators, Main Beam and Horn Control (2)

Direction indicators The switch operates the indicators only when the ignition is switched on.

Move the lever to position 'E' when turning left and to position 'F' when turning right.

After making a turn the signal is self-cancelled when the steering-wheel is returned to the straight-ahead position.

The switch lever may be held against spring pressure to select either left or right indicator and will cancel the indication immediately it is released without movement of the steering-wheel.

A visual warning of a front or rear bulb failure is given when, after switching on an indicator, the warning lamp and the serviceable bulb on the affected side give a continuous light.

Headlamp dipper With the headlamps switched on at the lighting switch, move the lever forward ('G') to use the main beams; the warning light will glow blue. Return the lever to the midway position to dip the beams.

Headlamp flasher Lift the lever towards the steering-wheel ('H') to flash the headlamps irrespective of whether they have been switched on at the lighting switch or not.

Horns Press the end of the lever inwards ('J') to sound the horns.

STARTING AND RUNNING INSTRUCTIONS

The following instructions are a guide for starting, running and loading the car, and include notes on the use of the controls and the indications of the instruments.

Running in The treatment given to a new car will have an important bearing on its subsequent life, and engine speeds during this early period must be limited. The following instructions should be strictly adhered to.

During the first 500 miles (800 km):
DO NOT exceed 45 m.p.h. (72 km/h).
DO NOT operate at full throttle in any gear.
DO NOT allow the engine to labour in any gear.

After the running-in period, speeds should be progressively increased up to maximum performance.

Choice of fuel Always use fuel with an octane rating best suited to your engine (see **'GENERAL DATA'**).

Filling up with fuel When filling up with fuel avoid filling the tank so that fuel is visible in the filler intake tube. Should this be done and the car left in the sun, there will be a considerable risk of fuel leakage due to expansion, and consequent danger from exposed fuel. If inadvertently overfilled and the car is to be parked, take care to park it in the shade with the filler intake as high as possible.

The fuel tank is vented through the filler cap. **UNIPART** market a lockable filler cap to fit this model.

Starting Check that the gear lever is in the neutral position.

If the engine is cold, pull out the mixture control (choke) and lock it in the desired position by turning the control knob a quarter of a turn clockwise. In extremely cold conditions it may be necessary to pull the control out to its fullest extent.

Switch on the ignition, check that the ignition warning light glows and that the fuel gauge registers, then operate the starter.

As soon as the engine starts, release the ignition key and warm up the engine at a fairly fast speed (see **'Warming up'**). Check that the oil pressure gauge is registering and that the ignition warning light has gone out. Unlock the mixture control (choke) and push it in completely as soon as the engine will run evenly without its use.

Starter Do not operate the starter for longer than five to six seconds.

To prevent damage the starter cannot be operated while the engine is running. If the engine fails to start, the ignition key must be returned to the 'off' position before the starter can be operated again.

If after a reasonable number of attempts the engine should fail to start, switch off the ignition and investigate the cause. Continued use of the starter when the engine will not start not only discharges the battery but may also damage the starter.

Mixture control (choke)
Fig. 1

The function of this control is to enrich the fuel/air mixture for cold engine starting and to provide a faster idle speed without enrichment during the warming-up period.

Pull out the mixture control knob (1) to the required position, turn the control knob **clockwise to lock.**

The amount which the control must be pulled out to achieve easy starting will be dependent on engine temperature.

Fig. 1

After the engine has started with the aid of the mixture control, unlock the control (turn it anti-clockwise) and push it in until only about ½ in (13 mm) of travel ('A') remains. With the control locked in this position the engine will run at a fast idle speed. Approximately one minute after starting, dependent on prevailing temperatures, return the mixture control fully.

Ignition warning light —Red
Fig. 1

The light (3) should glow when the ignition is switched on and go out when the engine has started. If the light does not go out, an incorrectly adjusted or broken alternator drive belt or other fault in the charging system is indicated.

Driving with the light glowing will quickly discharge the battery, especially if headlights and other electrical units are also in use.

Oil pressure gauge
Fig. 1

The gauge (2) should register a pressure as soon as the engine is started up. The pressure may rise above 80 lbf/in² (5·6 kgf/cm²) when the engine is started from cold and as the oil is circulated and warmed the pressure should then drop to between 50 and 80 lbf/in² (3·5 to 5·6 kgf/cm²) at normal running speeds and to approximately 10 to 25 lbf/in² (0·7 to 1·7 kgf/cm²) at idling speed.

Should the gauge fail to register any pressure, stop the engine immediately and investigate the cause. Start by checking the oil level.

Fig. 1

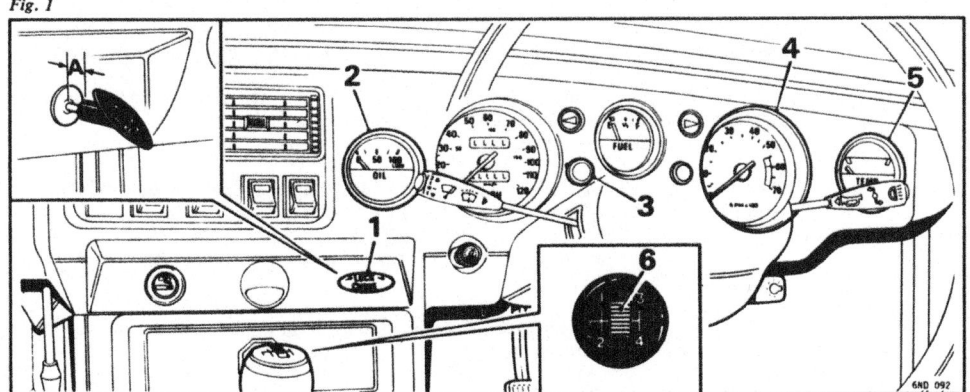

Starting and Running Instructions

Warming up Research has proved that the practice of warming up the engine by allowing it to idle slowly is definitely harmful. The correct procedure is to let the engine run fairly fast, approximately 1,000 rev/min., so that it attains its correct working temperature as quickly as possible. Allowing the engine to work slowly in a cold state leads to excessive cylinder wear, and far less damage is done by driving the car straight onto the road from cold than by letting the engine idle slowly in the garage.

Temperature gauge
Fig. 1 (5)

Normal operating temperature is reached when the pointer is midway (approximately) between 'C' cold and 'H' hot.

Overheating may cause serious damage. Should the pointer reach 'H' (hot), stop the engine and investigate the cause. Check the cooling fan operation (see page 45), the drive belt tension, and when the system has cooled, check the coolant level.

When the ignition is switched off the pointer returns to the 'C' (cold) position.

Tachometer
Fig. 1 (4)

For normal road work, and to obtain the most satisfactory service from your engine, select the appropriate gear to maintain engine speeds of between 2,000 and 4,500 rev/min.

When maximum acceleration is required upward gear selections should be made when the needle reaches the shaded sector (5,500–6,000 rev/min). Prolonged or excessive use of the highest engine speeds will tend to shorten the life of the engine. Allowing the engine to pull hard at low engine speeds must be avoided as this also has a detrimental effect on the engine.

The beginning of the red sector (6,000 rev/min) indicates the maximum safe speed for the engine.

Never allow the engine to enter the red sector.

Overdrive
Fig. 1

A slide switch (6) incorporated in the gear lever knob operates the overdrive and provides a higher driving ratio for use with third or fourth gear.

To engage the overdrive move the slide switch rearward; to disengage, move the slide switch forward. Accelerator pedal pressure should be maintained and it is not necessary to depress the clutch pedal during engagement or disengagement.

Overdrive can be engaged at any throttle opening when in third or top gear. If increased acceleration is required the overdrive can be 'switched out' without alteration to the throttle setting.

DO NOT switch out the overdrive when travelling at speeds exceeding the maximum obtainable in direct drive in third or fourth gear.

For maximum fuel economy use overdrive when cruising in top gear above 40 m.p.h. (64 km/h).

If for any reason the overdrive does not disengage, do not reverse the car otherwise extensive damage may result.

Wet brakes If the car has been washed, driven through water, or over wet roads for prolonged periods full braking power may not be available. Dry the brakes by applying the foot brake lightly several times while the car is in motion. Keep the hand brake applied while using high-pressure washing equipment.

On-tow for recovery Should it become necessary to tow the car, use the towing-eyes provided.

For recovery the car should be towed with the key in the ignition/steering lock at position 'I'. For tow starting the key should be at position 'II'.

Vehicle loading
Fig. 2 Due consideration must be given to the overall weight carried when fully loading the car. Any loads carried on a luggage rack (Tourer), or roof rack (GT), or downward load from a towing hitch must also be included in the maximum loading, see 'GENERAL DATA'.

Towing **The towing weight of 1,680 lb (762 kg) is the maximum that is permissible.** When using bottom gear a gradient of up to 1 in 8 can be ascended from rest while towing a weight not exceeding this figure. It may be necessary to adjust the maximum towing weight to comply with local conditions and regulations. The recommended downward load of a trailer or caravan on the towing hitch is 75 to 100 lb (34 to 45 kg), but this may be reduced or exceeded at the discretion of the driver.

UNIPART have designed a towing bracket and full electrical kit for your car. Be safe, be sure and fit **UNIPART** towing accessories.

Roof rack G.T. (accessory) Bulky rather than heavy **loads no greater than 50 lb (23 kg) may be carried on a roof rack.** Remember that any load on the roof may affect the handling of the car, especially in a cross wind or when cornering. Use the **UNIPART Roof Rack**.

Tyres The tyre loads and pressures must comply with regulations where such exist.

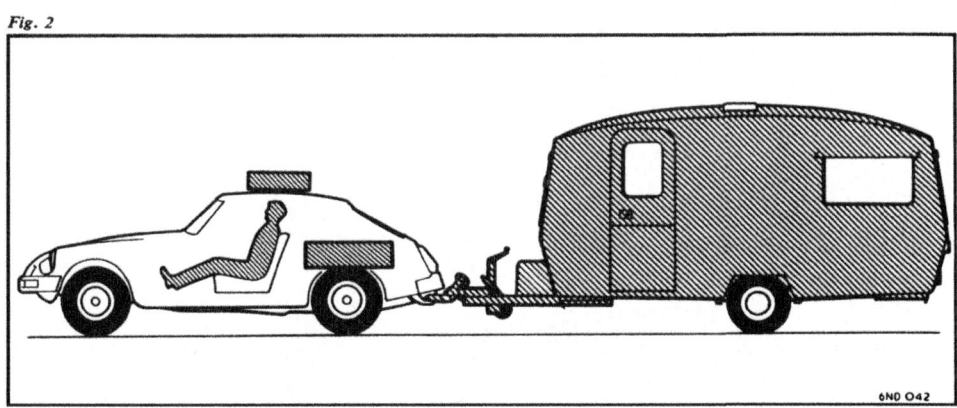

Fig. 2

LOCKS, FITTINGS AND BODY

Keys   Three keys and a duplicate set are provided, the large key for the steering lock/ignition switch, the larger all-metal key for the glovebox, and the small all-metal key for the doors and luggage compartment.

To reduce the possibility of theft the locks are not marked with a number. **NOTE THE KEY NUMBERS IMMEDIATELY** on taking delivery of the car, see page 5.

Window regulators
Fig. 1

To open a door window, turn the handle regulator (1) to obtain the opening required.

Door locks
Fig. 1

Both front doors may be locked from outside the car with the small key provided, and locked from inside the car with the door locking latch.

To unlock the front doors from the outside, insert the key into the lock and turn it towards the front of the car, return it to the upright position and withdraw it. Grasp the handle and depress the button (2) to open the door.

To lock the front doors from the outside, turn the key towards the rear of the car, return it to the upright position and withdraw it.

To lock the doors from inside the car, close the door and move the locking latch (3) towards the rear of the car. To open the doors, move the locking latch towards the front of the car and pull the release lever (4) rearwards. The doors can be opened from the outside when the locking latch is in the forward position. The locking latch cannot be set to the lock position while the door is open.

Fig. 1

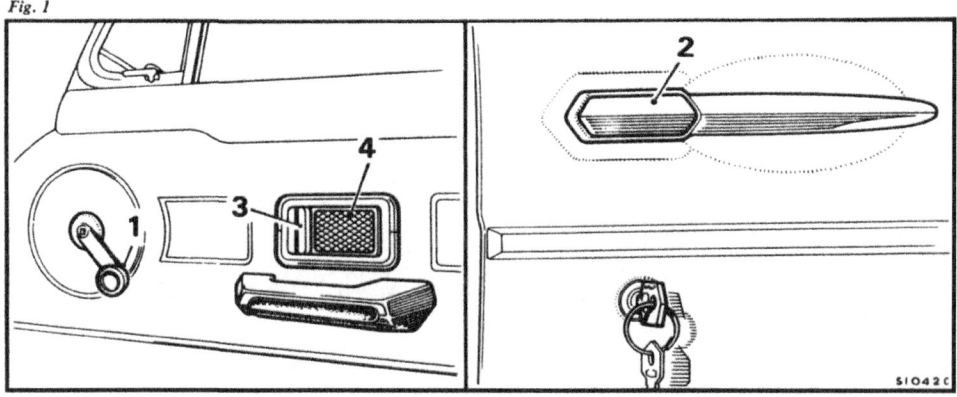

Glovebox
Fig. 2

To open, insert the key and turn it clockwise. Press the key and lower the lid, when unlocked press the centre of the lock to release the catch.

To lock, close the lid, turn the key anti-clockwise and withdraw it.

Luggage compartment
Fig. 3

To unlock, insert the key and turn it anti-clockwise.

To lock, turn the key clockwise and withdraw it.

Tourer. To open, depress the lock plunger and raise the lid. When fully raised the support stay will automatically spring into engagement and the lid will be held in the open position. Opening the luggage compartment lid automatically switches on the luggage compartment lamp.

To close the tourer luggage compartment, raise the lid slightly, push the catch (1) on the support stay forward to release the locking mechanism, and lower the lid. Closing the luggage compartment lid automatically switches off the luggage compartment lamp.

GT. To open, depress the lock plunger and raise the tailgate. Springs retain the tailgate in the open position. The interior lamp will automatically switch on as the tailgate is raised and switch off when the tailgate is lowered.

To close the GT tailgate apply light downward pressure at the lock.

WARNING: Exhaust fumes will be drawn into the car if it is driven with the luggage compartment lid open, causing a health hazard to the passenger and driver.

If it is imperative that the car be driven with the luggage compartment lid open, adverse effects can be minimized by adopting the following procedure:

1. Close all windows.
2. Open the face vents fully.
3. Set the heater controls to circulate the maximum amount of cold or hot air.
4. Switch on the blower motor.
5. Do not travel at high speed.

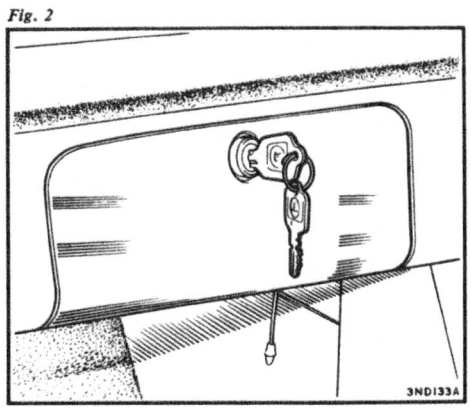

Fig. 2

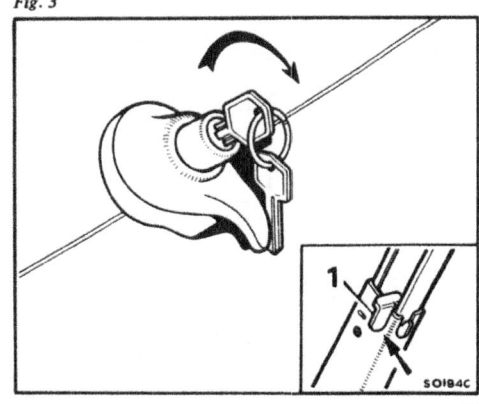

Fig. 3

Locks, Fittings and Body

Front ventilator windows
Fig. 4

To open, move the catch lever (1) upwards and push the window outwards.

To close, pull the catch inwards and then push it forward until the catch is in the locked position.

Rear ventilator windows
Fig. 5

To open, pull the catch (1) forward and then push the catch outwards.

To close, pull the centre of the catch inwards and then push it backwards until the catch snaps over into the locked position.

Bonnet
Fig. 6

To open, pull the knob (1) located inside the car on the left-hand side below the fascia panel. Press up the safety catch (2) under the front of the bonnet. Raise the bonnet and when fully raised the support stay will automatically spring into engagement and the bonnet will be held in the open position.

To close, raise the bonnet slightly, push the catch (3) on the bonnet stay rearwards to release the locking mechanism, and lower the bonnet. Apply light pressure with the palms of the hands at the front corners of the bonnet and press down quickly; undue force is not necessary and may cause damage. The safety catch and lock will be heard to engage.

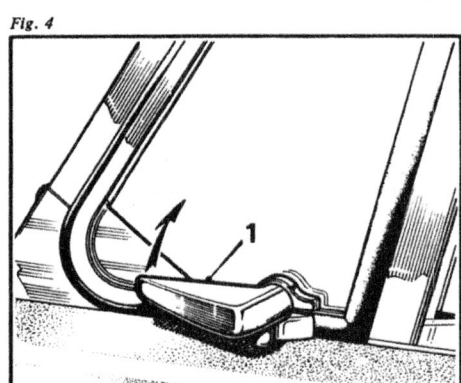
Fig. 4

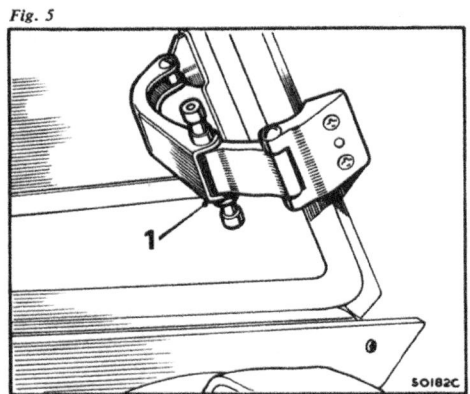
Fig. 5

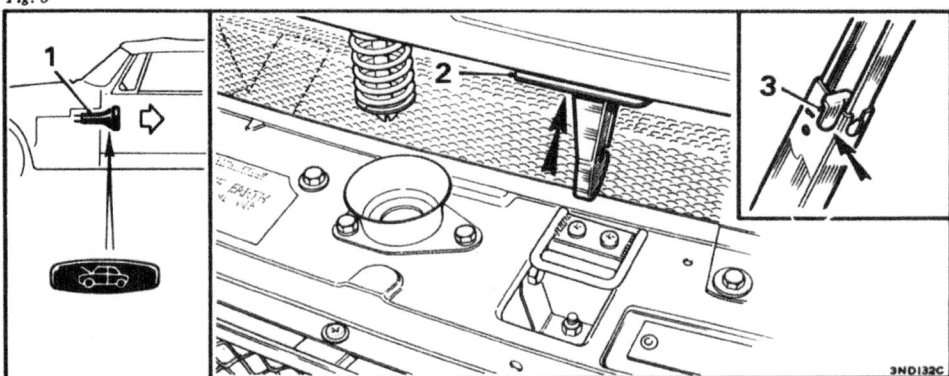
Fig. 6

Mirrors **Exterior** *Fig. 7*. The mirror head can be adjusted from the seat position when the window is open.

Interior *Fig. 8*. The mirror stem with anti-dazzle head is designed to break away from the mounting bracket on impact. The stem may be refitted in the mounting bracket as follows. Align the stem ball (1) with the bracket cup (2) ensuring that the small protrusion (3) on the stem aligns with the indent of the mounting bracket. Give the stem a smart tap with a soft instrument to join the two components.

Anti-dazzle *Fig. 8*. To reduce interior mirror dazzle, press the lever (4) towards the windscreen.

Arm-rest and ashtray *Fig. 9* To gain access to the compartment below the arm-rest, raise the forward end of the arm-rest. To empty the ashtray, raise the lid (1) and remove the ashtray by lifting under the stubber (2).

Do not attempt to remove the ashtray by pulling on the lid.

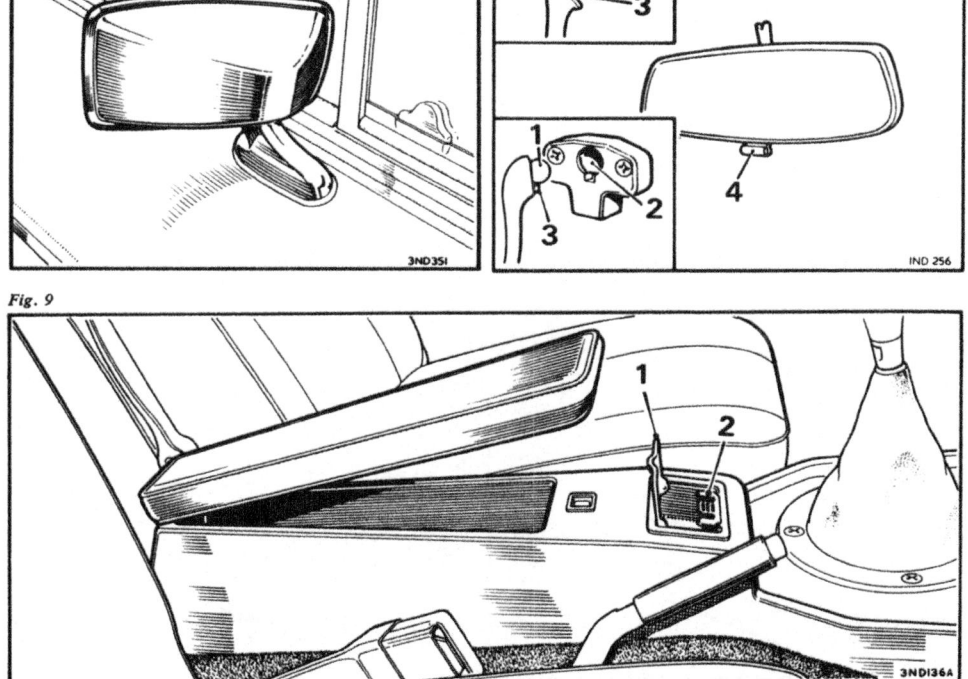

Fig. 7

Fig. 8

Fig. 9

Locks, Fittings and Body

Heated rear window (GT) (if fitted)
Fig. 10

The heated rear window has a heating element (arrowed) on the surface of the glass and with reasonable care will last indefinitely.

The following practices will damage the circuit and must be avoided.
1. Scratching off labels and advertising stickers.
2. Wiping the glass with the back of a ringed hand.
3. Stowing hard and metal objects so that they abrade the glass.
4. Cleaning with harsh abrasives.

Increased luggage area (GT)
Fig. 10

To increase the luggage capacity the back of the rear seat can be folded down.

Release the locks by moving the catch handles (1) downwards and moving the back of the seat (2) forward.

To return the seat to the normal position, lift the seat and lock in position by moving the catch handles upwards.

Bumpers
Spilling fuel on the bumper may cause temporary local swelling of the rubber. Remove stains by lightly wiping the whole of the bumper with petrol (fuel) or warm water and liquid detergent.

Fig. 10

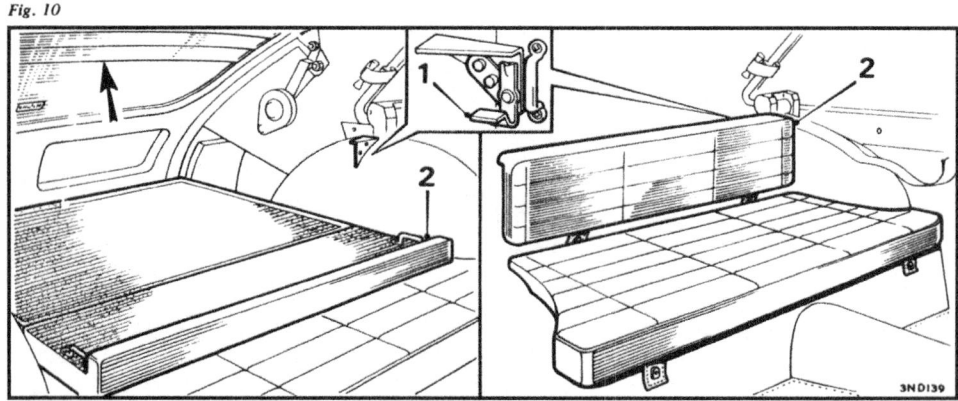

Body and door drainage points
Fig. 11

Periodic examination of the drain holes should be made to ensure that they are clear of obstruction; use a piece of wire to probe the apertures.

Careless application of underseal can result in restricted drainage. Masking tape or plugs used when underseal is being applied must be removed immediately the operation is completed.

Jacking up beneath the underfloor may deform the drain apertures; always use the jacking points provided.

Lubrication

To ensure trouble-free operation it is essential that the locks, hinges and catches are adequately lubricated.

Locks. Inject a small quantity of thin oil, preferably **Unipart Lockspray,** through the key slots and around the push-buttons. **Do not oil the steering lock.**

Hinges. Apply grease or oil to the joints of the hinges.

Bonnet catches. Apply grease to the moving surfaces of the bonnet release mechanism and oil to the release lever and safety-catch pivot points.

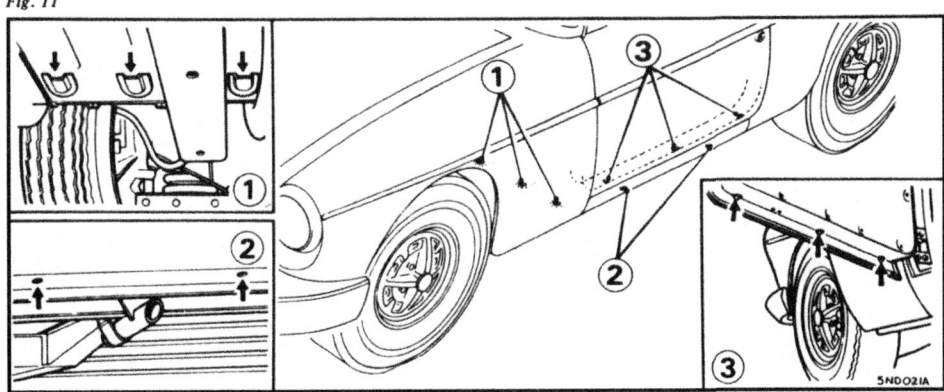

Fig. 11

Locks, Fittings and Body

It is most important that the instructions for raising, lowering and folding the hood are followed. Do not fold when the hood is wet or damp.

Lowering the hood
Fig. 12

CAUTION: Always ensure that the rear window is zipped in position before attempting to lower the hood.

Unclip the sun visors (1) and move them to one side.

Release both windscreen frame toggle catches (2).

Release the two fasteners (3) on the windscreen rails, the two fasteners (4) on the cant rails and the two fasteners (5) on the hood mounting brackets.

Fig. 13 Release the four fasteners from each rear quarter panel (6) and pull the hood slightly forward to disengage the hook (7) from the socket (8) on the body side panel.

Move the seat tilt catch forward and incline the seat backs towards the front of the car.

Fig. 14 Raise the hood header rail (11) until it is poised approximately midway over the door aperture.

Disengage the hood rear rail from the anchor plates (9) on the tonneau panel.

Release the rear belts from the quick-release fasteners on the tonneau panel, see page 28.

Fold each quarter-light (10) onto the back-light and continue the fold in the material forward to the header rail (11). **ENSURE THAT THE FOLD IS MADE IN THE HOOD MATERIAL BETWEEN THE QUARTER-LIGHT AND THE BACK-LIGHT. FAILURE TO DO THIS MAY CAUSE PERMANENT DAMAGE TO THE BACK-LIGHT MATERIAL.**

Push the header rail (11) rearwards, and at the same time draw the back-light and hood material (12) out over the luggage compartment lid ensuring that the hood material does not become trapped between the hood sticks.

Fig. 12

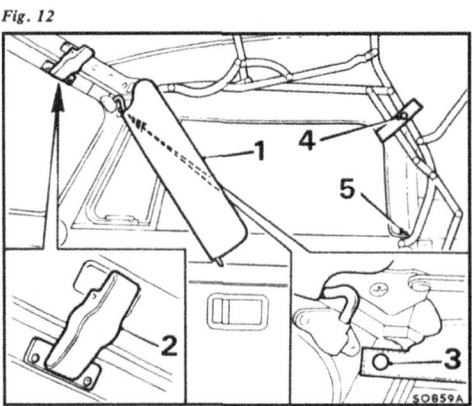

Fig. 13

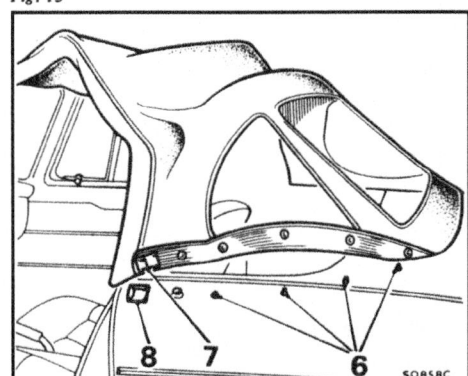

Fig. 15 Fully lower the hood. Fold the two windscreen frame toggle catches (13) rearwards to prevent them damaging the back-light.

Roll the rear window and hood material forward over the folded hood. Position and secure the two retaining straps (14).

Replace the sun visors and return the seat back-rests to their original positions.

Fit the hood or tonneau cover and secure the seat belts to the quick-release fasteners.

Raising the hood
Fig. 12, 13, 14 and 15

Remove the hood or tonneau cover, and release the seat belts from the quick-release fasteners on the tonneau panel.

Move the seat catch forward and incline the seat back towards the front of the car.

Unclip the sun visors (1) and move to one side.

Release the two retaining straps (14) and unfold the rear window and hood material rearwards over the luggage compartment.

Raise the header rail (11) and unfold the hood. Engage the rear rail in the anchor plates (9). Pull the hood slightly forwards and engage each hook (7) in its socket (8) on the body side panel. Position the header rail on the windscreen ensuring the rail seal is forward of the seal flange. Secure the windscreen frame toggle catches and fasteners (3), (4), and (5) inside the car.

Secure the fasteners (6) at each rear quarter.

Secure the seat belts to the quick-release fasteners.

Reposition the seats and sun visors.

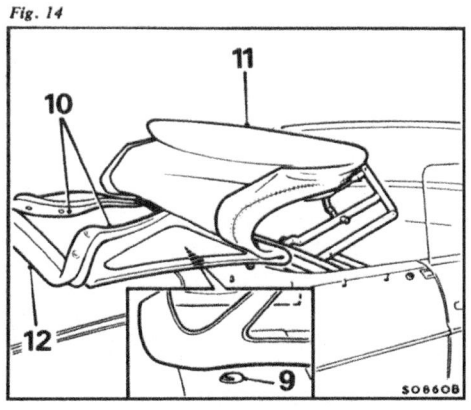

Fig. 14

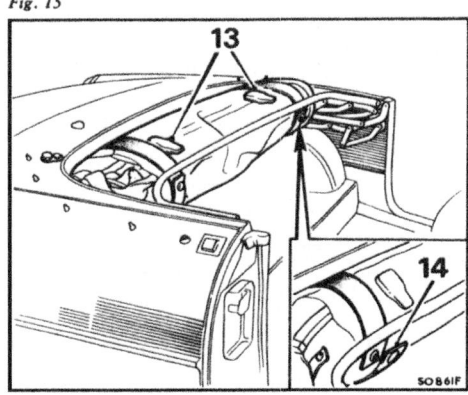

Fig. 15

Locks, Fittings and Body

Rear window The rear window may be folded down when extra ventilation is required with the hood in the raised position.

Undo the zip, moving it around the rear window to the left-hand side of the hood.

Fold the window panel down, avoiding creasing or buckling the transparent window material.

CAUTION: It is important that the rear window is zipped in position before lowering the hood. Failure to do this may cause permanent damage to the rear window material.

Fitting the hood cover
Figs. 16 and 17

Assemble the hood cover support rail (15) and fit it into the hood support sockets with the cross-rod towards the rear.

Lay the hood cover over the support rail and thread the seat belt quick-release fasteners (16) through the two small holes in the hood cover.

Engage the hood cover rear rails in the anchor plates (17) on the tonneau panel.

Pull the cover slightly forwards and engage each side hook in its socket (18) on the body panel.

Secure the fasteners (19) at each quarter side panel.

Secure the four fasteners (20) inside the car.

Secure the seat belts to the quick-release fasteners.

Removing the hood cover Reverse the fitting procedure.

Fig. 16

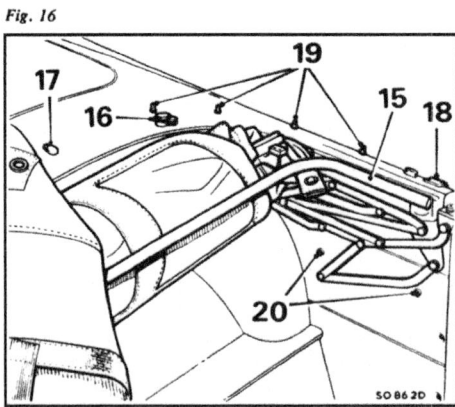

Fig. 17

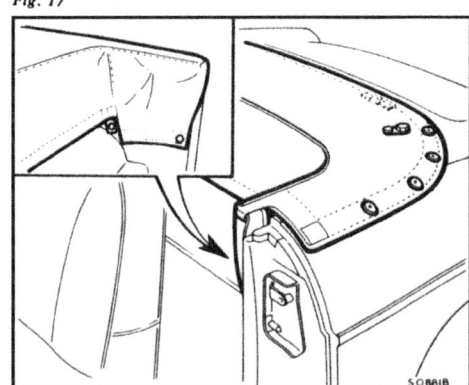

Tonneau cover
Fig. 16 and 18

Fitting. Assemble the hood cover rail (15) and fit it into the hood support sockets with the cross-rod towards the rear.

Lay the tonneau cover over the cockpit and thread the seat belt quick-release fasteners (16) through the two small holes in the tonneau cover.

Engage the tonneau cover rear rails in the anchor plates (17) on the tonneau panel. Place the pockets in the tonneau cover over the head restraints on the seats; it may be necessary to adjust the seat back (see page 23), to align the pockets in the cover with the head restraints.

Secure the tonneau cover to each rear quarter with the four fasteners (19), and the fastener (21) on the cover at the cut-away.

With the zip undone, extend the tonneau cover forward, fitting the forward pocket over the steering wheel and securing to the fasteners (22) on each windscreen pillar, and the fastener (23) on the fascia panel top. Zip up the cover.

Fig. 18 Usage. The centre zip allows the cover to be folded down to give access to the driving seat or both seats. Undo the zip, release the press-studs on the fascia, and the two press-studs (21 and 24) at the cut-away. Fold the cover down and inwards behind the seat (arrowed). Move the seat tilt catch forward, and incline the seat back towards the front of the car. Secure the tonneau cover with the fasteners (25) on the flap to the heel board. Return the seat back-rests to their original position. Secure the seat belts to the quick release fasteners.

Removing. Reverse the fitting procedure.

Stowage Stowage bags are provided to protect the hood cover and hood cover rail. The stowage bags together with the tool bag are stowed in the luggage compartment and secured with the straps provided.

Fig. 18

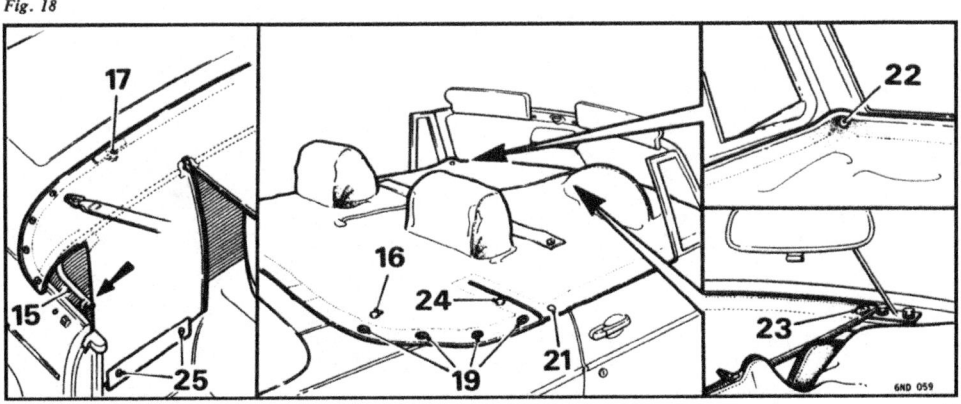

Locks, Fittings and Body

Hard top **Fitting.** Remove the hood. Fit the hard top side brackets into the hood support sockets and secure with the bolts and spring washers.

Position the hard top on the car, engaging the rear securing plates with the slotted anchor plates on the tonneau panel (inset, Fig. 19) ensuring that the sealing rubber does not foul the slots.

Line up the hard top drip moulding with the rear wing top beading. Push the hard top forwards and engage the toggle catch tongues in the sockets on the windscreen frame.

Fit the bolts into the side fixing brackets; screw in but do not tighten. Ensure that the front sealing rubber is correctly positioned forward of the windscreen frame. Adjust the toggle catches to give adequate tension (when fastened the securing bolt slots allow movement), tighten the securing bolts, fasten the catches and lock them with the securing clips (inset, Fig. 20).

Check that the sealing rubbers are correctly positioned, then slowly and evenly tighten the side fixing bolts until the hard top seals evenly to the body. **AVOID OVERTIGHTENING.** Measure the gap between the hard top and body side fixing brackets (arrowed, Fig. 19). Remove the bolts and fit washers between the brackets to the thickness of the gap. Refit and tighten the bolts.

Wind up both windows and check that a gap of approximately $\frac{5}{16}$ in. exists between the rear edge of the window and the hard top quarter channel. Adjust if necessary by loosening the side fixing bolts and repositioning the hard top. Ensure that there is an adequate seal between the window and hard top rubber and that the doors, when opened with the windows up, do not foul the opening surround.

Removing. Unlock and release the windscreen toggle fasteners. Remove the side fixing bolts. Raise the front of the hard top to disengage the toggle fastener tongues from the windscreen sockets, move the hard top to the rear to disengage the anchor plates, then lift it clear of the car. Remove the side fixing brackets from the hood support sockets. Assemble the fittings loosely to the hard top to prevent loss.

Fig. 19

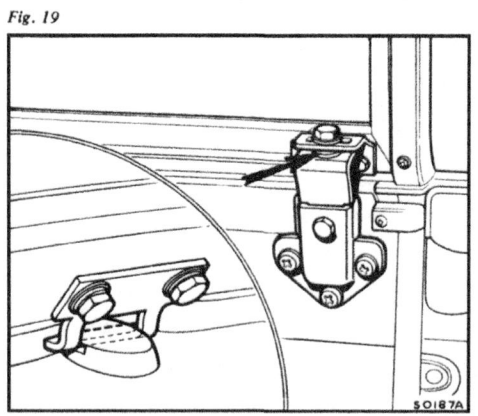

Fig. 20

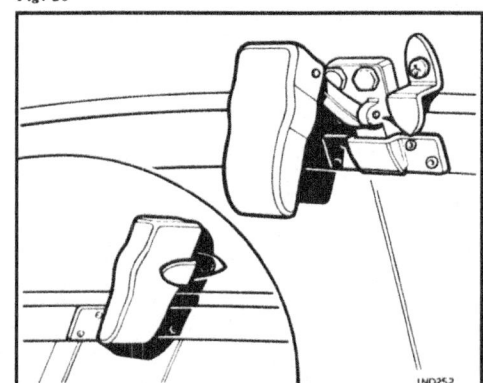

SEATS AND SEAT BELTS

SEATS

Seat adjustment
Fig. 1
Front seats can be moved forwards or backwards if the lever (1) located beneath the front of each seat is pressed outwards; hold the lever in this position while the seat position is adjusted. The locking pin is spring loaded and will automatically lock the seat in the required position when the lever is released.

Adjustable back-rest
Fig. 1
The angle of the seat back-rest may also be adjusted by easing the body weight from the seat back-rest, and moving the lever (2) in the direction of the arrow. Release the lever and ensure the seat is locked in position by applying back pressure.

Access to rear seats
Fig. 1
Move the seat catch (3) forward, and fold the back of the front seat forwards. The catch will automatically re-engage when the rear of the seat is moved back to the correct driving position.

Head restraint
Fig. 1
The head restraint (4) may be raised or lowered as desired.

To remove, lift the head restraint to its stop and withdraw by rocking it from side to side whilst pulling upwards.

SEAT BELTS

Warning system The seat belt warning system functions when the ignition/starter switch is operated.

The **'FASTEN BELTS'** warning lamp will flash continuously each time the ignition/starter switch is operated, if the driver's seat belt is not fastened.

Fig. 1

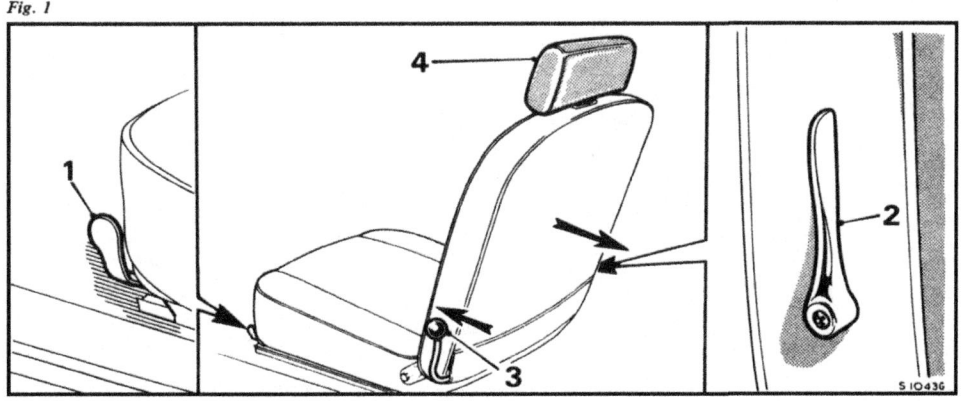

Seats and Seat Belts

Wearing — **Always wear a belt as a complete lap and diagonal assembly** and never at any time wear it loosely, as this reduces its protection. Ensure that the belt is lying flat and is not twisted. Always stow a seat belt that is not in use.

Never attempt to use a seat belt for more than one person, even for small children.

Rear fixing (Tourer)
Fig. 2
The long belt is attached at the rear end by a quick-release fastener to the tonneau panel.

To release, press down the black plastic locking plate (1) and slide the belt bracket (2) out of engagement with the securing stud slot.

To secure, position the large hole in the belt bracket over the securing stud, slide the bracket forward until it engages in the securing stud slot and locks in position with the locking plate. Check that the belt webbing is not twisted.

Hood and tonneau covers (Tourer)
Holes are provided in the hood cover and tonneau cover to accommodate the seat belt quick-release fasteners mounted on the tonneau panel. After fitting the hood cover or tonneau cover attach the seat belts to the fasteners.

Seat belt (Tourer)
Fig. 2
To fasten, lift the engagement tongue (3) and draw the belt over the shoulder and across the chest. Push it into the locking clip (4) of the short belt nearest the wearer.

To adjust, tilt the edge of the adjuster (5) upwards and pull the webbing through until the belt is comfortably tight. Slide the end of the belt (6) along the webbing to take up any slack after final adjustment.

To release, press the release button (7) on the short belt.

To stow, after releasing the belt, push the tongue into the parking pocket (8).

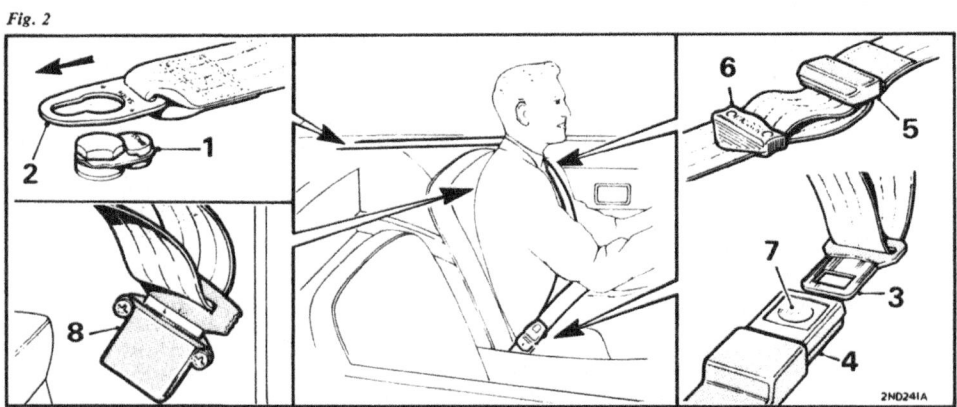

Fig. 2

Seat belt GT
Fig. 3

To fasten, lift the engagement tongue (2) from the parking device and draw the belt over the shoulder and across the chest. Push it into the locking clip (3) of the short belt nearest the wearer.

To release, press the release button (4) on the short belt.

To stow, after releasing the belt allow the webbing to retract into the automatic reel (1). Fit the engagement tongue in the parking pocket (6). To prevent the tongue sliding down the belt, ensure that the slide (5) is close to the tongue when the belt is stowed in the parking device.

Testing. WARNING—This test must be carried out under safe road conditions, i.e. on a dry, straight metalled road, during a period when the road is free from traffic. With the belts in use, drive the car at 5 m.p.h. (8 km.p.h.) and brake sharply. The automatic locking device should operate and lock the belt. It is essential that the driver and passenger are sitting in a normal relaxed position when making the test. The retarding effect of the braking must not be anticipated. If a belt fails to lock, consult your Distributor or Dealer.

Care of the belts

No unauthorized alterations or additions to the belts should be made. Inspect the webbing periodically for signs of abrasion, cuts, fraying, and general wear; pay particular attention to the fixing points and adjusters.

Do not attempt to bleach the belt webbing or re-dye it. If the belts become soiled, sponge with warm water using a non-detergent soap and allow to dry naturally.

Do not use caustic soap, chemical cleaners or detergents for cleaning: do not dry with artificial heat or by direct exposure to the sun.

Renew a seat belt assembly that has withstood the strain of a severe impact.

Fig. 3

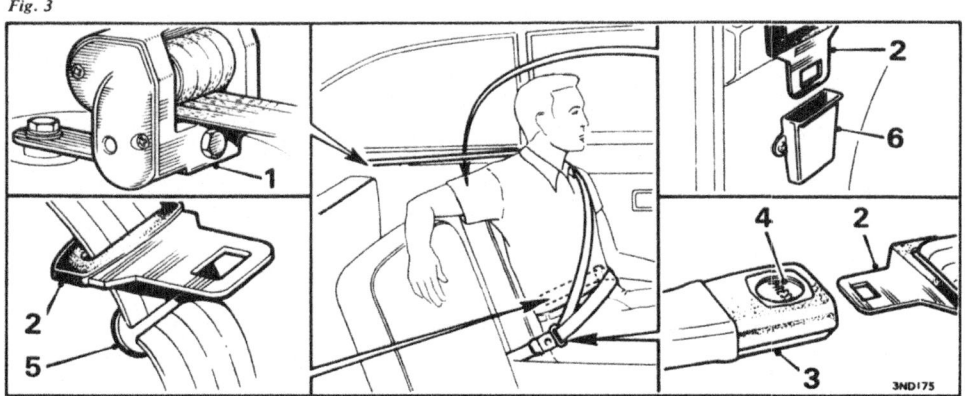

HEATING AND VENTILATING

Fresh air Fresh air is admitted to the car for cooling and ventilation through an adjustable
Fig. 1 vent mounted behind the centre console.

Air enters the car interior through the two doors (1) located one each side of the gearbox tunnel in the foot wells.

The flow of air may be adjusted by moving the control knob (2) backwards to one of the three open positions; move the knob to the most forward position to close the vent.

Face-level Fresh unheated air for cooling and ventilation from the face-level vents on the
vents fascia can be obtained by turning the serrated controls wheels (3) of each vent
Fig. 1 downwards to open the vents.

Move the shutter control knob (4) mounted in the centre of each vent horizontally and vertically to direct the air flow as required.

Fresh-air The heating and ventilating system is designed to provide fresh air either heated
heater by the engine cooling system or at outside temperature to the car at floor level
Fig. 1 and for demisting and defrosting to the windscreen. Full heat output is not available until the engine has reached normal operating temperature.

Air distribution for heating is independent of the fresh-air system; the control knob (2) (in Fig. 1) should be in the closed position (fully forward) when heated air is being distributed.

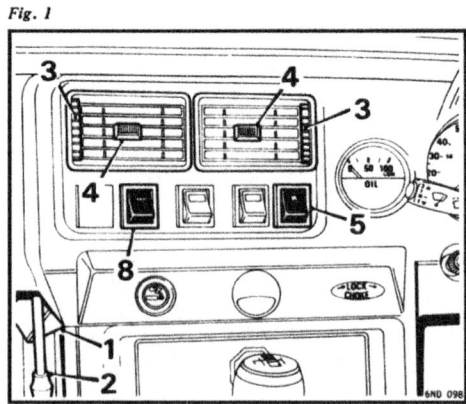

Fig. 1

Heater controls
Fig. 1 and 2

Air temperature. Turn the knob (6) anti-clockwise to the arrow end of the blue sector for unheated air supply. Further anti-clockwise movement will progressively increase the temperature, with maximum heat output at the 'HOT' end of the red sector.

Air distribution. Turn the knob (7) anti-clockwise to 'INTERIOR', air supply is distributed to the car interior at the foot wells, with reduced air flow to the windscreen. Further anti-clockwise movement of the knob to 'DEFROST'; all air is directed to the windscreen.

Booster blower. The booster blower operates when the ignition is switched on. Press the lower end of the switch rocker (5) to the central position to operate the blower at slow speed. Press the switch rocker fully down to boost the air flow at fast speed.

Usage
The heater and air flow controls may be set at the position marked on the control knobs or to any other intermediate positions. By varying the control settings, and utilizing the booster blower, a wide range of settings can be obtained to suit prevailing conditions.

Illumination
The control dials and the position indicators on the rotary control knobs together with the green illumination light on the face of the blower switch are illuminated when the panel lights are switched on.

Heated rear window (GT) (if fitted)
Fig. 1
The heated rear window will operate only when the ignition is switched on. The green illumination light on the face of the switch (8) glows when the panel lights are switched on. Notes on the use of the heated rear window can be found under **'LOCKS, FITTINGS AND BODY'**.

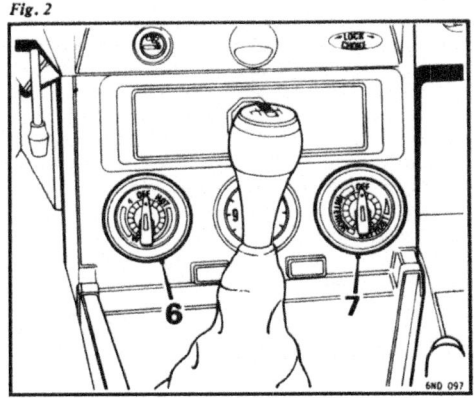

Fig. 2

CLEANING

Interior   **Carpets:** Clean with a semi-stiff brush or a vacuum cleaner, preferably before washing the outside of the car. Occasionally give the carpets a thorough cleaning; dilute one part **UNIPART Upholstery Cleaner** with eight parts warm water, apply vigorously with a semi-stiff brush and wipe over with a damp sponge or cloth. Carpets must not be 'dry-cleaned'.

Plastic faced upholstery: Clean with diluted upholstery cleaner. Spot clean with **UNIPART Upholstery Cleaner** spread thinly over the surface with a brush or cloth, leave for five minutes, then wipe over with a damp sponge or cloth.

Nylon faced upholstery: Remove loose dirt with a brush or vacuum cleaner. The nylon pile has been chemically treated to resist soiling and care must be taken when cleaning. Use **Unipart Nylon Cleaner**. To remove a stain, apply the cleaner, then pat and wipe with a clean cloth in the direction of the pile until the stain is removed. **DO NOT RUB**. When dry, gently brush against the pile, then with the pile.

Body   Regular care of the body finish is necessary if the new appearance of the car exterior is to be maintained against the effects of air pollution, rain, and mud.

Wash the bodywork frequently, using a soft sponge and plenty of water containing **UNIPART Car Shampoo**. Large deposits of mud must be softened with water before using the sponge. Smears should be removed by a second wash in clean water, and with the sponge if necessary. When dry, clean the surface of the car with a damp chamois-leather. In addition to the regular maintenance, special attention is required if the car is driven in extreme conditions such as sea spray or on salted roads. In these conditions and with other forms of severe contamination an additional washing operation is necessary which should include underbody hosing. Any damaged areas should be immediately covered with paint and a complete repair effected as soon as possible. Before touching-in light scratches and abrasions with paint, thoroughly clean the surface. Use petrol/white spirit (gasoline/hydrocarbon solvent) to remove spots of grease or tar.

The application of **UNIPART Hi-shine Car Polish** is all that is required to remove traffic film and to ensure the retention of the new appearance.

Bright trim   Never use an abrasive on stainless, chromium, aluminium, or plastic bright parts and on no account clean them with metal polish. Remove spots of grease or tar with petrol/white spirit (gasoline/hydrocarbon solvent) and wash frequently with water containing **UNIPART Car Shampoo**. When the dirt has been removed polish with a clean dry cloth or chamois-leather until bright. Any slight tarnish found on stainless or plated components which have not received regular attention may be removed with **UNIPART Chrome Cleaner**. An occasional application of light mineral oil or grease will help to preserve the finish, particularly during winter when salt may be used on the roads, but these protectives must not be applied to plastic finishes.

Windscreen   If windscreen smearing has occurred it can be removed with **UNIPART Glass Cleaner**.

UNIPART products mentioned above are obtainable from your Distributor or Dealer.

COOLING SYSTEM

Fig. 1   The pressurized cooling system incorporates an expansion tank, making the need for regular topping-up unnecessary. The expansion tank, connected to the top of the radiator, receives the normal overflow of coolant when the system is in the process of heating up. When the temperature of the system drops, the pressure in the radiator is reduced and the overflow then returns to the radiator.

Cooling fan   For information on the electrically driven cooling fan see page 45.

Checking   The coolant level must only be checked when the system is **COLD.** Remove the expansion tank cap to check the coolant level which must be maintained to the half-full point of the tank.

If coolant is not displaced or the level in the expansion tank has fallen appreciably since the last periodical check, a leak in the cooling system or overheating must be suspected.

Topping-up   **WARNING: As injury could be caused while the system is hot by escaping steam
*Fig. 1***   **or coolant the filler plug (1) must not be removed before the pressure relief cap (2).**

If the system is hot, protect the hands against escaping steam, turn the expansion tank pressure relief cap (2) slowly until the stop is felt and allow the pressure in the system to escape gradually, then remove the cap. Add coolant to the expansion tank to the half-full point, and refit the cap. Remove the filler plug (1) and add coolant to bring the level to the top of the filler neck; refit the plug.

Fig. 1

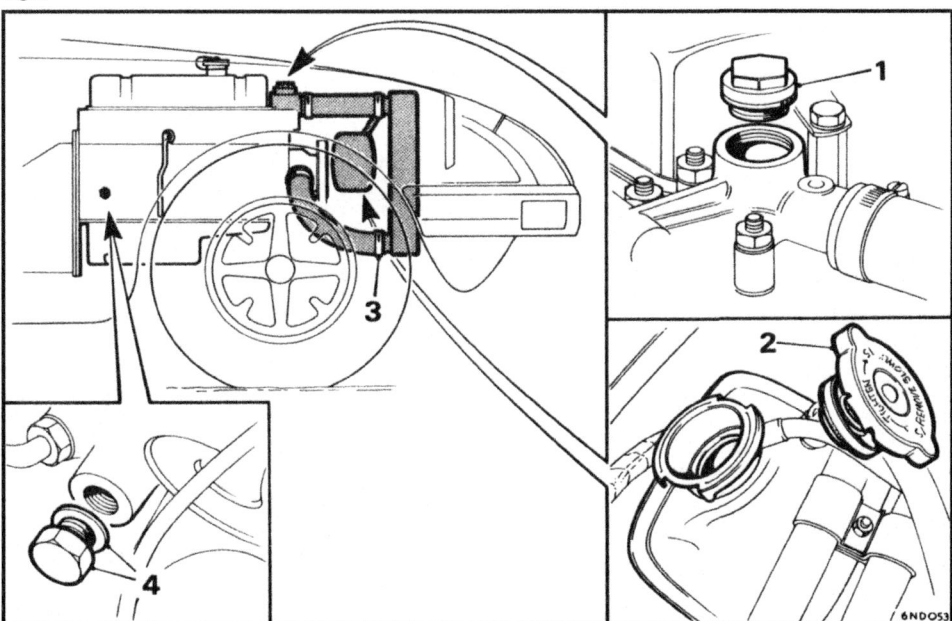

Cooling System

Draining To drain the cooling system, stand the car on level ground, remove the expansion
Fig. 2 tank cap (2), and the filler plug (1) from the coolant outlet elbow. Slacken the hose clip and disconnect the bottom hose (3) at its connection to the radiator. Remove the drain plug (4) on the cylinder block.

Collect the coolant in a clean container if it is to be used again as cars are filled with a 33⅓ per cent solution of anti-freeze before they leave the factory.

Leave a reminder on the vehicle to the effect that the cooling system has been drained.

Owing to the location of the car heater and the expansion tank they cannot be drained with the cooling system. Anti-freeze must be used in the cooling system when freezing conditions are likely to be encountered.

Filling Refit the bottom hose and close the engine drain tap. Check that all hose connec-
Fig. 2 tions are tight. Turn the heater temperature control knob to 'HOT' to open the heater valve.

Top up the coolant in the expansion tank so that the tank is half-full. Refit the cap (2).

Fill the system through the filler neck and bring the level up to the bottom of the threads. Refit the filler plug (1).

Fig. 2

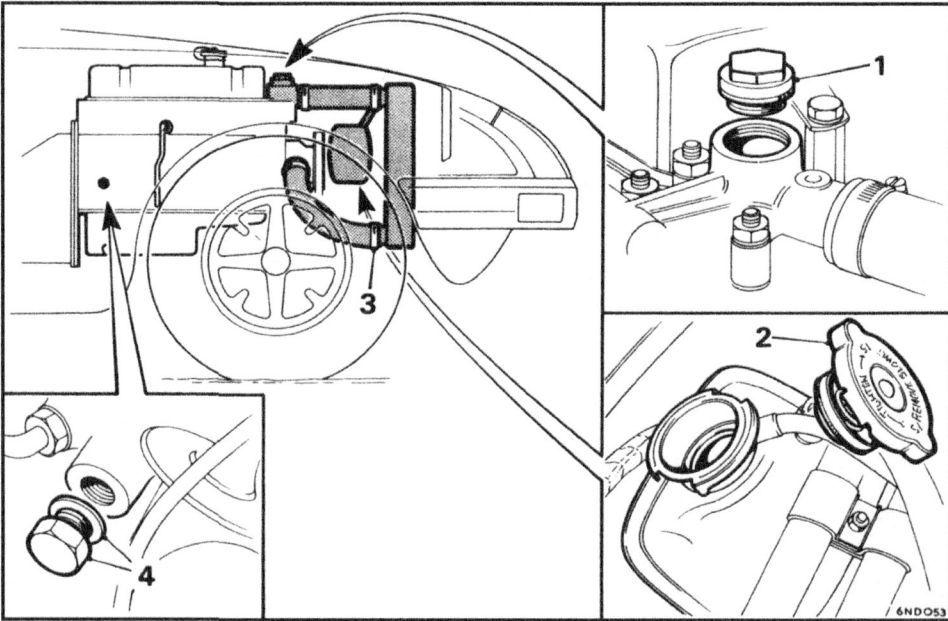

Start up and run the engine until the top radiator hose is warm, and switch off the engine.

Turn the expansion tank cap to its safety stop to release the pressure, and if necessary top up the expansion tank to half-full. Refit the cap.

Remove the radiator filler plug and top up once more to the bottom of the threads. Refit the filler plug.

CAUTION: The system operates at a pressure of 15 lb/in^2 (1 kg/cm^2) and the figure **15** is marked on the expansion tank cap (2).

Frost precautions
Water expands when it freezes, and if precautions are not taken there is considerable risk of bursting the radiator, cylinder block, or heater. The heater unit cannot be drained with the cooling system; it is therefore essential to use anti-freeze in the cooling system in freezing conditions.

We recommend the use of **Bluecol U universal** anti-freeze to protect the cooling system.

If Bluecol U universal is not available any anti-freeze conforming to specification B.S. 3151 or B.S. 3152 may be used. Anti-freezes to these specifications are compatible with Bluecol U universal and can be used with it. Bluecol U universal should not be mixed with other universal anti-freezes.

After filling with anti-freeze solution, attach a warning label to a prominent position on the car stating the type of anti-freeze contained in the cooling system to ensure that the correct type is used for topping-up.

Anti-freeze can remain in the cooling system for two years provided that the specific gravity of the coolant is checked periodically and anti-freeze added as necessary. The specific gravity check should be carried out by an authorized Distributor or Dealer. After the second year the system should be drained and flushed by inserting a hose in the filling orifice and allowing water to flow through until clean. Make sure that the cooling system is water-tight, examine all joints and replace any defective hose with a new one. Refill with the appropriate anti-freeze solution, and add 0·25 pint (0·2 litre) of neat anti-freeze to the expansion tank.

The recommended quantities of anti-freeze solution are given below.

Do not use radiator anti-freeze solution in the windscreen-washing equipment. Use the correct washer solvent, which will not damage the paintwork.

Anti-freeze	Commences to freeze		Frozen solid		Amount of anti-freeze		
%	°C	°F	°C	°F	Pts	U.S. Pts	Litres
25	−13	9	−26	−15	$2\frac{7}{8}$	$3\frac{1}{2}$	1·6
$33\frac{1}{3}$	−19	−2	−36	−33	$3\frac{7}{8}$	$4\frac{5}{8}$	2·2
50	−36	−33	−48	−53	$5\frac{3}{4}$	7	3·3

WHEELS AND TYRES

Jacking up
Fig. 1

The jack is designed to lift one side of the car at a time. Apply the hand brake and block the wheels on the opposite side to that being jacked; use a wood block jammed tight against the tyre tread.

Remove the jack socket plug. Insert the lifting arm (1) of the jack into the socket located in the door sill panel. **Make certain that the jack lifting arm is pushed fully into the socket and that the base of the jack is on firm ground.** The jack should lean slightly outwards at the top to allow for the radial movement of the car as it is raised.

WARNING: Do not work beneath the vehicle with the lifting jack as the sole means of support. Place suitable supports under the front side-members or rear axle to give adequate support and safety while working.

Jack maintenance

If the jack is neglected it may be difficult to use in a roadside emergency. Examine it occasionally, clean off accumulated dust, and lightly oil the thread to prevent the formation of rust.

ROAD WHEELS

Wheel nuts

Owners are recommended to check the wheel nuts for tightness each week in addition to checking the other items listed. Take care not to overtighten. Torque wrench setting 60 to 65 lbf ft (8·3 to 9 kgf m).

Pressed type
Removing and refitting
Fig. 1

Slacken the four nuts securing the road wheel to the hub; turn anti-clockwise to loosen and clockwise to tighten. Raise the car with the jack to lift the wheel clear of the ground and remove the nuts. Withdraw the road wheel from the hub.

When refitting the road wheel locate the wheel on the hub, lightly tighten the nuts (2) with the wheel nut spanner (securing nuts must be fitted with the **taper side towards the wheel**), and lower the jack. Fully tighten the wheel nuts, tightening them diagonally and progressively, at the same time avoid over-tightening.

The wheel centre trim (3) must be removed and fitted to the wheel in use.

Replace the wheel disc and the jack socket plug.

Fig. 1

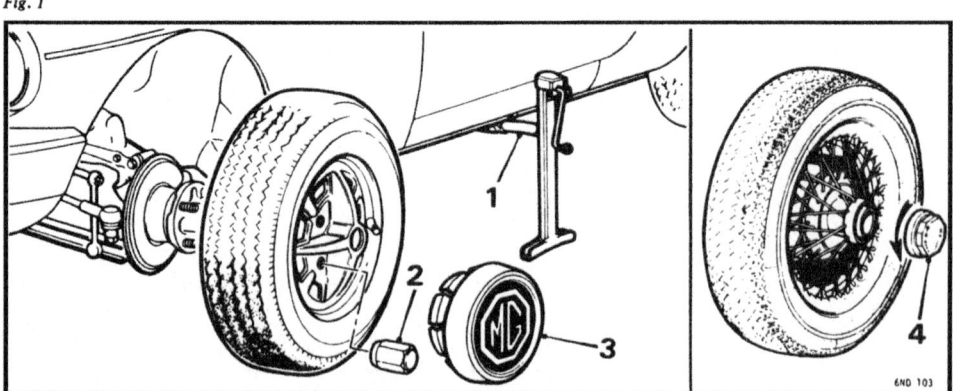

Wire type (if fitted)
Removing and refitting
Fig. 1

Use the spanner and hammer to slacken and tighten the octagonal hub nuts (4).

Always jack up a wheel before using the tools, and always tighten the hub nuts fully.

Hub nuts (4) are marked 'LEFT' or 'RIGHT' to show which side of the car they must be fitted, and also with the word 'UNDO' and an arrow.

Before replacing a wheel wipe all serrations, threads, and cones of the wheel and hub and then lightly coat them with grease. If a forced change is made on the road, remove, clean, and grease as soon as convenient.

Maintenance

When the car is new, after the first long run or after 50 miles of short runs, jack up the wheels and use the hammer and spanner to make sure that the nuts are tight.

Spare wheel
Figs. 2 and 3

The spare wheel is secured to the floor of the luggage compartment on tourer cars and below the luggage compartment floorboard on GT cars. To gain access to the spare wheel on GT cars (Fig. 3) turn back the luggage compartment floor covering, unscrew the two quick-release screws (1) and lift the floorboard (2).

Unscrew the clamp plate (3) to release the spare wheel.

When refitting, position the wheel in the well of the luggage compartment and retain in position with the clamp plate.

The spare wheel tyre on new cars is inflated above the recommended running pressure. The pressure must be checked and adjusted before use.

TYRES

Markings

Tyres are marked with the maximum load and inflation pressure figures. When fitting replacement tyres ensure that they are to the same specification and marking. **The permissible load and tyre pressures are shown on pages 65 and 66 of this handbook.**

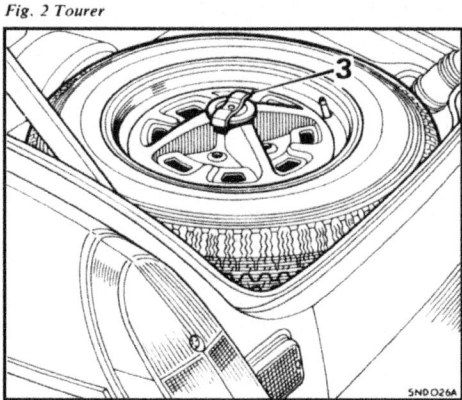

Fig. 2 Tourer

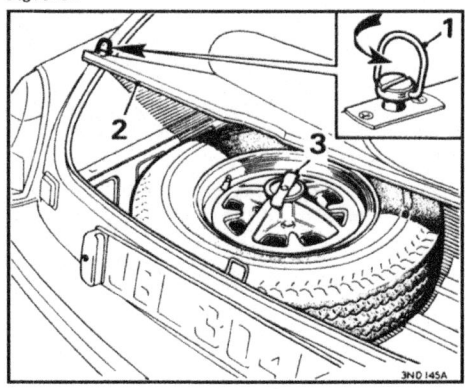

Fig. 3 GT

Wheels and Tyres

Tyre pressures Owners are reminded that tyre wear and inflation pressures may be subject to legal requirements; check the tyre pressures weekly, including the spare, and adjust if necessary to the recommendations given in 'GENERAL DATA'. The spare tyre should be maintained at the highest recommended pressure and adjusted before use.

Pressures should be checked with the **UNIPART Tyre Pressure Gauge** when the tyres are cold, and should not be reduced in warm tyres where the increase above normal pressure is due to temperature. Tyres are permeable and a natural pressure loss will occur with time. The pressure loss in a week should be no more than 2 lbf/in^2 (0·14 kgf/cm^2); any unusual pressure loss should be investigated. If necessary use a **UNIPART Foot Pump to increase the pressure.**

Driving with under-inflated tyres can be hazardous and causes rapid tyre wear and possible permanent damage to the cords of the tyre casing.

Valves and caps See that the valve caps are screwed down firmly by hand. Do not use tools as too much force will damage the rubber seating. The cap prevents the entry of dirt into the valve mechanism and forms an additional air seal on the valve.

Tyre care The tyres should also be inspected at frequent intervals for damage and wear. Excessive local distortion as a result of striking a kerb, a loose brick, a deep pothole, etc., may cause the casing cords to fracture. Every effort should be made to avoid such obstacles.

Any oil or grease which may get onto the tyres should be cleaned off by using petrol (fuel) sparingly. Do not use paraffin (kerosene), which has a detrimental effect on rubber.

Flints and other sharp objects should be removed with a penknife or similar tool. If neglected, they may work through the tyre.

Tubeless tyres Normally a tubeless tyre will not leak as a result of penetration by a nail or other puncturing object, provided that it is left in the tyre. At a convenient time have the tyre removed for vulcanizing. If a small diameter puncture has been made a temporary repair can be carried out with the tyre manufacturer's plugging kit.

NOTE: The insertion of a plug to repair a puncture in a tubeless tyre must be regarded as a temporary measure and a **permanent vulcanized repair must be made as soon as possible.** In no circumstances should a plug repair be made to the side wall of a tyre.

The instructions given for the temporary repair of tubeless tyres must be disregarded when tubes are fitted. If in any doubt, consult your Distributor/Dealer.

Wheel and tyre balance Unbalanced wheel and tyre assemblies may be responsible for abnormal wear of the tyres and vibration in the steering. Consult your Distributor/Dealer.

Wheel assemblies should always be refitted on the same axle and in the position in which they were balanced.

BRAKES AND MASTER CYLINDERS

Front brake pads
Fig. 1

Wear on the disc brake friction pads (indicated) is automatically compensated for during braking operations and manual adjustment is therefore not required.

If the wear on one pad is greater than on the other their operating positions should be changed over by your Distributor or Dealer.

Remove the road wheel to gain clear access to the pads for inspection.

The pads must be renewed when the lining material has worn to the minimum permissible thickness of $\frac{1}{16}$ in (1·6 mm) or will have done so before the next regular inspection is due. Special equipment is required to renew the brake pads; this work should be entrusted to your Distributor or Dealer.

After fitting new pads, within the limits of safety, heavy braking should be avoided for a few days to allow the pads to bed-in.

Rear brakes
Fig. 2

Excessive brake pedal travel is an indication that the rear brake-shoes require adjusting. The brake-shoes on both rear wheels must be adjusted to regain even and efficient braking.

Adjusting. Chock the front wheels, fully release the hand brake and jack up each rear wheel in turn placing suitable supports beneath the vehicle—see **'WARNING'** on page 36. Turn the adjuster (1) in a clockwise direction (viewed from the centre of the car), using a **UNIPART Brake Adjusting Spanner** until the brake-shoes lock the wheel, then turn the adjuster back until the wheel is free to rotate without the shoes rubbing. Repeat the adjustment on the other rear brake.

Hand brake
Fig. 2

The hand brake is automatically adjusted with the rear brakes. If there is excessive movement of the hand brake lever, consult your authorized Distributor or Dealer.

To lubricate, charge the nipple (2) on the hand brake cable with one of the recommended greases.

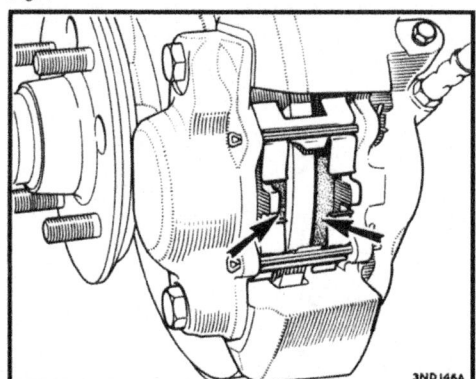

Fig. 1

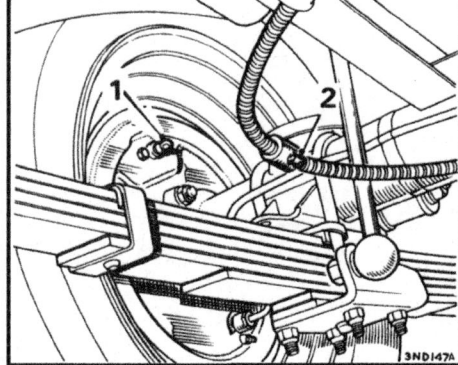

Fig. 2

Brakes and Master Cylinders

Replacing brake-shoes and pads When it becomes necessary to renew the brake-shoes or pads it is essential that only **genuine** replacements, with the correct grade of lining, are used. Always fit new shoes as complete axle sets, never individually or as a single wheel set. Serious consequences could result from out-of-balance braking due to mixing of linings.

Replacement brake-shoes are obtainable from your Distributor or Dealer under the **Service Exchange Scheme,** see page 73.

Inspecting rear brake linings
Fig. 3
Chock the front wheels and release the hand brake. Jack up each wheel in turn, placing suitable supports beneath the vehicle—see **'WARNING'** on page 36.

Remove the road wheel and slacken the brake-shoe adjuster.

Remove the two countersunk screws (1) and withdraw the brake-drum (2).

Inspect the linings (3) for wear, and clean the dust from the backplate assembly and drum, preferably using methylated spirit (denatured alcohol). Brake lining dust is dangerous to health if inhaled and therefore should not be blown from the drums. Make certain that sufficient lining material remains to allow the car to run until the next regular inspection is due without the thickness falling below the safe limit.

Refit the brake-drums and road wheel, and adjust the brake-shoes.

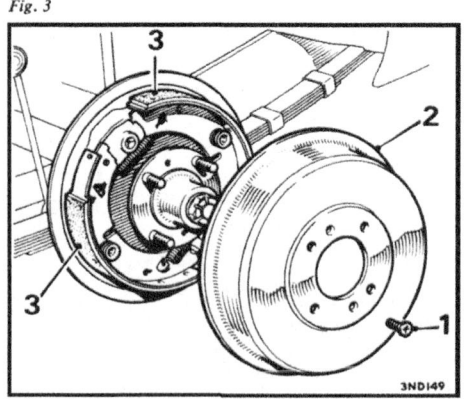

Fig. 3

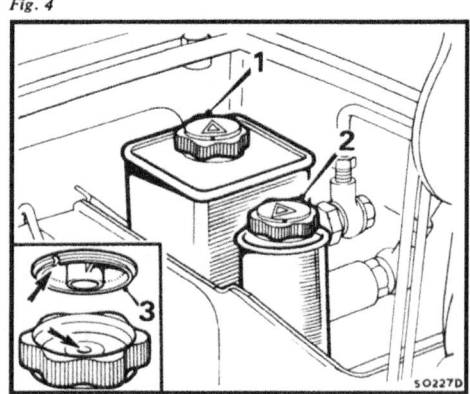

Fig. 4

Brake and clutch master cylinder
Fig. 4

To check the level of the fluid in the brake (1) and clutch (2) master cylinder reservoirs, remove the plastic filler caps.

The fluid level must be maintained up to the bottom of the filler neck.

Top up if necessary with **UNIPART 550 Brake fluid;** alternatively use a high-boiling-point brake fluid conforming to specification S.A.E. J1703c with a minimum boiling point of 260°C (500°F). **DO NOT use any other type of fluid** Frequent topping-up is indicative of a leak in the system which must be checked and the leak rectified immediately.

Before refitting the filler caps, separate the dome (3) from the filler cap and check that the breather holes, indicated by arrows, are clear. Snap fit the dome onto the filler cap.

NOTE: Brake fluid can have a detrimental effect on paintwork. Ensure that fluid is not allowed to contact paint-finished surfaces.

Brake pedal
Fig. 5

A free movement of $\frac{1}{8}$ in (3 mm) (A), measured at the pedal pad must be maintained on the pedal. To adjust the free movement, slacken the stop light switch locknut (1) and turn the switch (2) clockwise to decrease or anti-clockwise to increase the clearance. Tighten the stop light switch locknut.

Servo filter
Fig. 6

The filter should be cleaned at the recommended intervals with compressed air at low pressure. Do not use cleaning fluid or lubricant of any description on the filter.

Removing the filter. Lever the dome (1) off the valve cover, remove and clean the filter (2).

When refitting, ensure that the valve spring (4) is securely located onto the valve, and the seal (2) is located in the head of the dome (1). Refit the filter (3) and snap the dome onto the cover.

Fig. 5

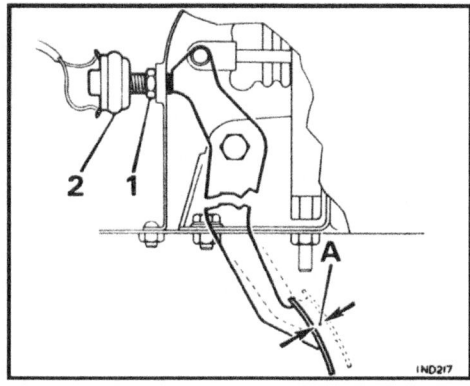

Fig. 6

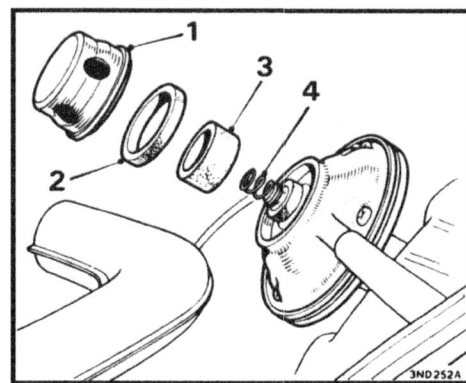

Brakes and Master Cylinders

Visual check Examine the clutch and brake hoses, pipes, unions, and joints for tightness and general condition. It is most important to ensure that no chafing of connections or pipes develops at any time, and that leakages are rectified immediately.

Preventive maintenance In addition to the recommended periodical inspection of brake components it is advisable as the car ages, and as a precaution against the effects of wear and deterioration, to make a more searching inspection and renew parts as necessary.

It is recommended that:

(1) Disc brake pads, drum brake linings, hoses, and pipes should be examined at intervals no greater than those laid down in the Passport to Service.

(2) Brake fluid should be changed completely every 18 months or 18,000 miles (30000 km) whichever is the sooner.

(3) All fluid seals in the hydraulic system should be renewed, and all flexible hoses should be examined and renewed if necessary every 3 years or 36,000 miles (60000 km) whichever is the sooner. At the same time the working surface of the piston and of the bores of the master cylinder, wheel cylinders, and other slave cylinders should be examined and new parts fitted where necessary.

Care must be taken always to observe the following points:

(*a*) At all times use the recommended brake fluid.

(*b*) Never leave fluid in unsealed containers. It absorbs moisture quickly and this can be dangerous if used in the braking system in this condition.

(*c*) Fluid drained from the system or used for bleeding is best discarded.

(*d*) The necessity for absolute cleanliness throughout cannot be over-emphasized.

ELECTRICAL

POLARITY The electrical installation on this car is **NEGATIVE** (−) earth return and the correct polarity must be maintained at all times. Reversed polarity will permanently damage semi-conductor devices in the alternator and tachometer, and the radio transistors (when fitted).

Before fitting a radio or any other electrical equipment, make certain that it has the correct polarity for installation in this car.

BATTERY

Access
Fig. 1

Release the rear seat cushion securing straps from the fasteners, and pull the cushion forward.

Remove the carpet covering the rear compartment floor. Turn the three quick-release fasteners (1) anti-clockwise one half turn and remove the battery compartment cover panel (2).

Checking topping-up
Fig. 1

The car must be on level ground when the electrolyte is being checked.

DO NOT USE A NAKED LIGHT WHEN CHECKING THE LEVELS and do not use tap water for topping-up.

Remove the battery vent cover; use the grip at the centre of the cover (3), this will ensure that the filling valves are operated correctly. If no electrolyte is visible inside the battery, pour distilled or de-ionized water into the filling trough (4) until the six tubes (5), and the connecting trough (6), are filled. Refit the vent cover.

The above operations should not be carried out within half an hour of the battery having been charged, other than by the car's own generating system, lest it floods. In extremely cold conditions run the engine immediately after topping-up so as to mix the electrolyte.

IMPORTANT: The vent cover must be kept closed at all times, except when topping-up. The electrolyte will flood if the cover is removed for long periods during or within thirty minutes of the battery being normal (6·5 amp) charged. Single-cell discharge testers cannot be used on these batteries. Operation of the filling device will be destroyed if the battery case is drilled or punctured.

Fig. 1

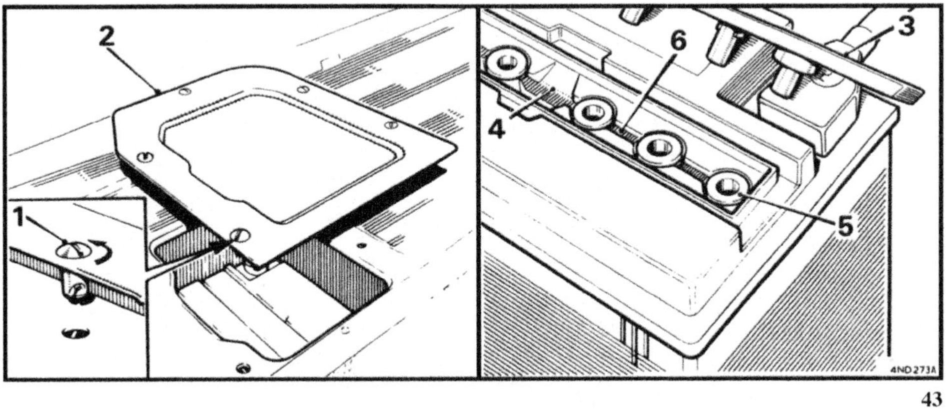

Electrical

General maintenance The batteries must be kept dry and clean; cable and battery terminals should be smeared with petroleum jelly.

Do not leave the battery in a discharged state for any length of time. When not in regular use have the battery fully charged, and every four weeks give a short refresher trickle charge to prevent permanent damage to the battery plates.

BATTERY BOOSTING AND CHARGING

CAUTION: The following precautions must be observed to avoid the possibility of serious damage to the charging system or electrical components of the vehicle.

Battery boosting
Fig. 2
When connecting an additional battery to boost a discharged battery in the vehicle, ensure that:

— the booster battery is of the same nominal voltage as the vehicle battery;

— the interconnecting cables are of sufficient capacity to carry starting current;

— **the cables are interconnected one at a time and to the booster battery first;**

— the cables are connected between the battery terminals in the following order: first, + (positive) to + (positive) and then − (negative) to − (negative);

— the engine speed is reduced to 1,000 rev/min or below before disconnecting the boost battery. The vehicle battery must never be disconnected while the engine is running.

Battery charging When charging the battery in the vehicle from an outside source such as a trickle charger, ensure that:

— the charger voltage is the same as the nominal voltage of the battery;

— the charger positive (+) lead is connected to the positive (+) terminal of the battery;

— the charger negative (−) lead is connected to the negative (−) terminal of the battery.

ALTERNATOR The following precautions must be observed to prevent inadvertent damage to the alternator and its control equipment.

Polarity. Ensure that the correct battery polarity is maintained at all times: reversed battery or charger connections will damage the alternator rectifiers.

Battery connections. The battery must never be disconnected while the engine is running.

For drive belt tension and alternator cleaning see page 57.

RADIATOR COOLING FAN
Fig. 3

The electrically driven cooling fan mounted in front of the radiator is controlled by a thermostatic switch (1) on the radiator top tank. During normal driving the fan will operate infrequently, but when driving slowly or running the engine when stationary it will operate more often.

Checking Switch on the ignition. Pull the connector (2) from the thermostatic switch, press the leads (3) together and the fan should operate.

Re-connect the leads, start and run the engine until normal operating temperature is reached and continue running the engine until the fan operates; this should occur before the temperature gauge pointer has reached the 'H' (hot) red sector.

Should the fan not operate in the manner described in either of the above two checks, consult your Distributor or Dealer.

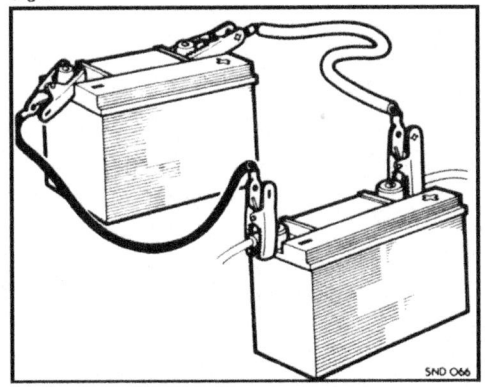
Fig. 2

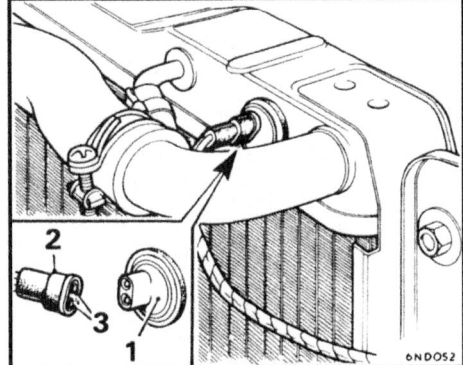
Fig. 3

Electrical

FUSES The fuses are housed under the fuse cover (1) mounted in the engine compartment on the right-hand wing valance.
Fig. 4

Fuse connecting 1–2. The fuse (2) protects one parking lamp, one tail lamp, and one number-plate lamp.

Fuse connecting 3–4. The fuse (3) protects one parking lamp, one tail lamp, and one number-plate lamp.

Fuse connecting 5–6. The fuse (4) protects the circuits which operate only when the ignition is switched on. These circuits are for the direction indicators, brake stop lamps, reverse lamps and seat belt warning, brake warning, temperature and fuel gauges, and the heated rear window (if fitted).

Fuse connecting 7–8. The fuse (5) protects the circuits which operate independently of the ignition switch, namely horns, interior and luggage compartment lamps, headlamp flasher, and the radio (if fitted).

Line fuses **Hazard warning—brown wiring.** The 17 amp continuous current rated (35 amp blow rated) line fuse (7) protects the hazard warning lamps.
Fig. 4

Fan thermostat—white/brown and green wiring. The 17 amp continuous current rated (35 amp blow rated) line fuse (8) protects the fan thermostat circuit.

Radio. A separate additional line fuse protects the radio (if fitted). See the instructions supplied with the radio for the correct fuse ratings.

To change a line fuse, hold one end of the cylindrical fuse holder (9); push in and twist the other end (10). Remove the fuse (11) from the cylindrical holder.

Spare fuses Two spare fuses (6) are provided and it is important to use the correct replacement fuse. The fusing value, current rated 17 amp continuous (35 amp blow rated), is marked on a coloured slip of paper inside the glass tube of the fuse.
Fig. 4

Fig. 4

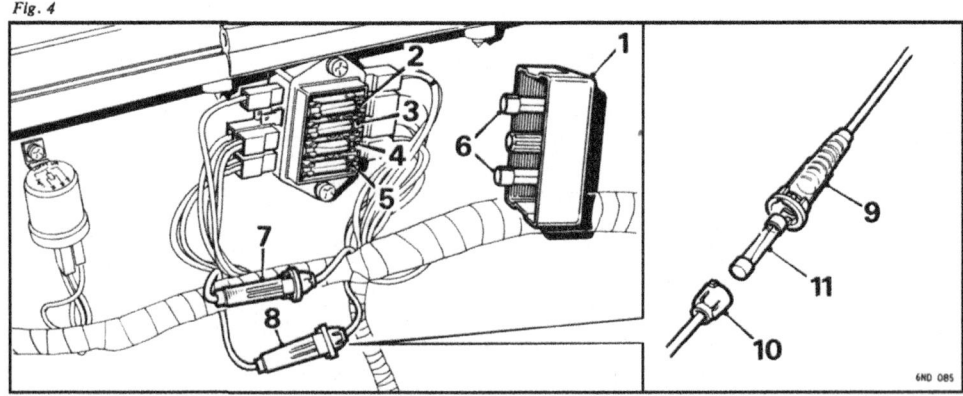

Blown fuses A blown fuse is indiated by the failure of all the units protected by it, and is confirmed by examination of the fuse when withdrawn. Before renewing a blown fuse inspect the wiring of the units that have failed for evidence of a short-circuit or other fault.

Accessories If an electrical accessory is being fitted and it is required to operate independently
Fig. 4 of the ignition circuit it should be connected to terminal '8' on the fuse block; if it is required to operate only when the ignition is switched on, connect it to terminal '6'. The terminal numbers are marked on the fuse block.

HEADLAMPS
Light unit Removing. Ease the bottom of the outer rim (1) forward away from the lamp.
Fig. 5 Unscrew the three inner rim retaining screws (2), remove the inner rim (3), withdraw the light unit (4) and disconnect the three-pin socket (5) from the bulb. Remove the seal (6) and at the same time withdraw the pilot lamp bulb holder (7) from the back of the light unit, release the spring (8) and withdraw the bulb (9) from the reflector seating.

CAUTION: Do not touch the bulb glass with the fingers; wipe it clean using a cloth moistened with industrial alcohol (methylated spirit).

Refitting. Fit the bulb into the reflector seating, ensuring that the spigots engage in the slots on the light unit. Fit the spring, ensuring that it registers as shown (10) over the spigots of the bulb and underneath the retaining spigots of the light unit. Fit the pilot lamp bulb holder into the back of the light unit, press the seal into place and re-connect the three-pin socket.

Position the light unit in the headlamp body, ensuring that the three lugs formed on the outer edge of the light unit engage in the slots formed in the headlamp body. Fit the inner retaining rim. Position the outer rim on the retaining lugs with the join of the rim at the bottom of the lamp, press the rim downwards and inwards.

Beam setting Two adjusting screws are provided on each headlamp for setting the main beams. The screw (11) is for adjusting the beam in the vertical plane, and the screw (12) is for horizontal adjustment. The beams must be set in accordance with local regulations; resetting and checking should be entrusted to your Distributor or Dealer, who will have special equipment available for this purpose.

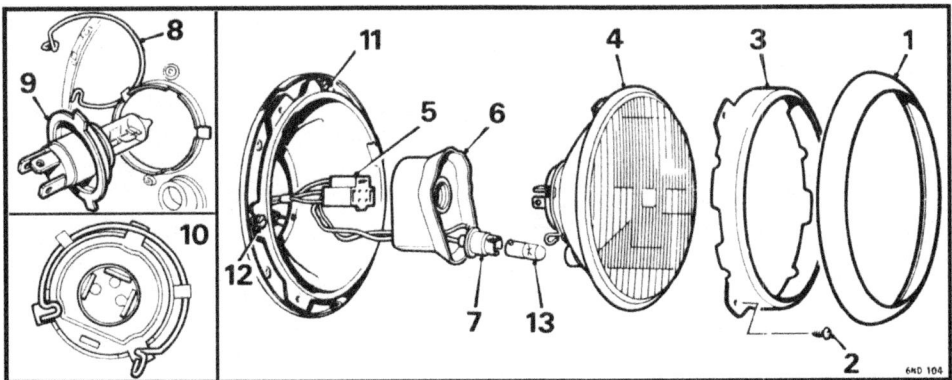

Fig. 5

Electrical

LAMPS

Pilot
Fig. 5
The pilot lamp bulbs are incorporated in the headlamps. To gain access to the bulb, remove the light unit (4) and disconnect the three-pin socket (5). Lift the bottom of the seal (6), and withdraw the pilot lamp bulb holder (7) from the light unit. Press in and turn the bulb (13) to release it from the bulb holder.

Direction indicator
Fig. 6
To gain access to the direction indicator bulb, unscrew the two retaining screws (2) and withdraw lens (1).

The bulbs have a bayonet-type fixing.

Ensure that the seal is in place on the lamp body and the fibre washers are under the head of the screws.

Stop, tail and direction indicator
Fig. 7
Remove the lens retaining screws (1) and slide the lens upwards to gain access to the direction indicator (2) and stop/tail (3) bulbs.

The direction indicator lamps have a single filament bulb (2) which may be fitted either way round in the socket. The tail and stop lamp bulb (3) has a twin filament and offset bayonet fixing to ensure correct replacement.

Reverse
Fig. 8
To renew a bulb remove the two securing screws (1) and withdraw the lens. Press the bulb (2) down towards the lower contact and withdraw it from the lamp.

Fit one end of the new bulb into the hole in the lower contact, then press the top of the bulb into the lamp until the point of the cap engages in the hole in the upper contact.

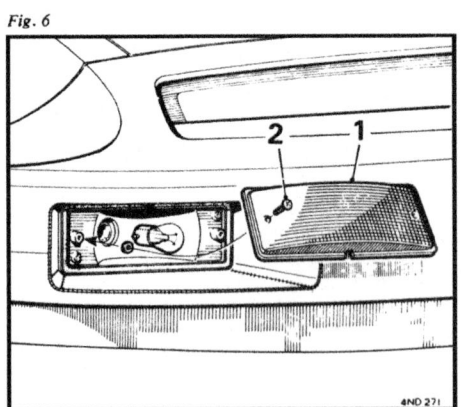

Fig. 6

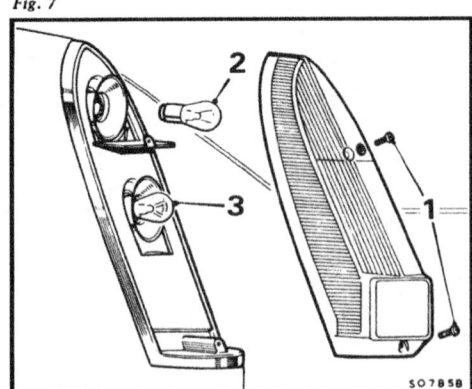

Fig. 7

Number-plate Slacken the screw (1), remove the metal cover (2) and glass lens (3). Press in and
Fig. 9 turn the required bulb to release it from the bulb holder. When refitting, ensure
the glass lens engages over the raised portion at each side of the seal and that
the sealing washer is fitted to the cover retaining screw.

Tailgate or The plastic lens on the interior lamp is held in position by four locating lugs.
interior (GT) To gain access to the bulb, gently squeeze the lens sides and pull outwards.
Fig. 10 Withdraw the festoon-type bulb from the retaining clips.

Luggage The lens is held in the lamp by four locating lugs. To gain access to the bulb,
compartment gently squeeze the sides of the lens together and withdraw it from the lamp.
lamp (Tourer) The bulb may then be withdrawn from its contacts.
Fig. 11

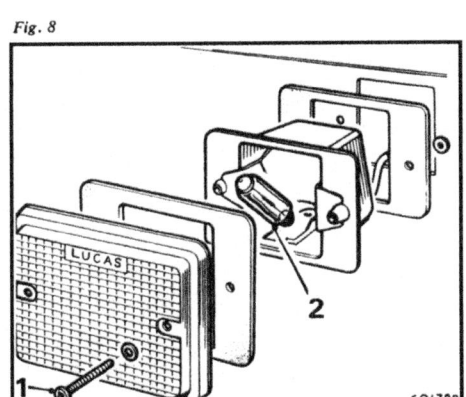
Fig. 8

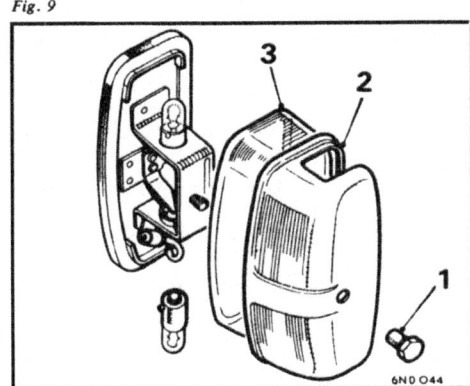
Fig. 9

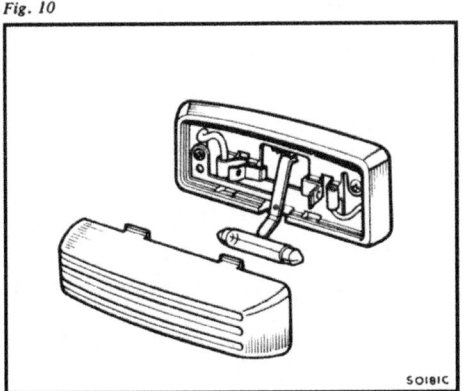
Fig. 10

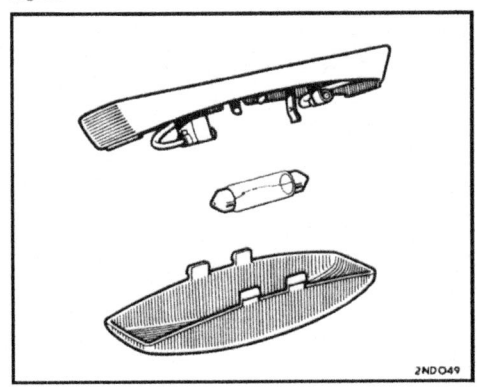
Fig. 11

Electrical

Fascia warning and illumination lamps
Fig. 12

The warning, instrument panel and switch illumination lamps on the fascia are located in the positions shown. The warning and instrument lamp bulb holders are accessible from below the fascia.

Instrument panel lamps. To change a bulb, remove the push-fit bulb holder (1) from the back of the instrument and unscrew the bulb (2). To remove the oil gauge illumination bulb the centre console must also be withdrawn to give access.

Warning lamp bulbs. To change a bulb, remove the push-fit bulb holder (3) from the back of the warning lamp and remove the bulb (4) which has a bayonet type fitting.

Switch illumination. To change a bulb, remove the switch cover (5) by engaging a suitable wire clip into the forward recess on each side of the cover and pull the cover from the switch. To remove the blower switch, interior lamp switch or heated back light switch illumination bulb (6) use a wiring harness connector cover or a suitable length of rubber tube to unscrew the bulb. To remove the hazard warning switch, illumination bulb (7) release the spring clip (8) and remove the bulb.

Centre console warning and illumination lamps
Fig. 13

To gain access to the bulbs the centre console must be withdrawn.

To withdraw the centre console. Unscrew the four screws (10), noting that the front screw is the shortest, and remove the gaiter retaining ring (11). Raise the hinged arm-rest and unscrew the retaining screw (12). Remove the arm-rest (13) by easing it up over the gaiter and the gear lever. Remove the four screws (14) retaining the console and withdraw the console (15) rearwards to give the required access to change a bulb.

Fig. 12

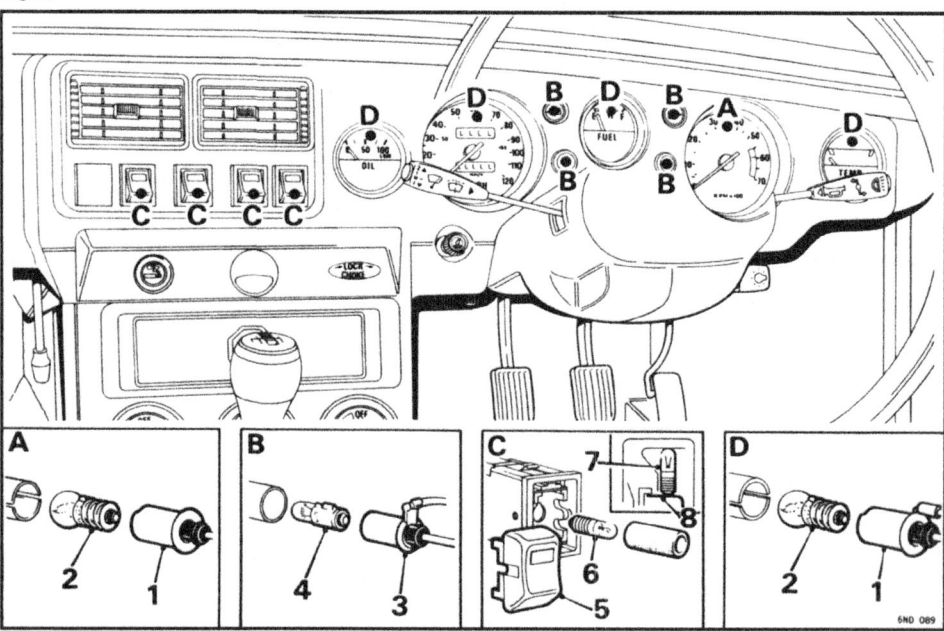

Courtesy light and clock illumination. To change a bulb, withdraw the centre console for access, remove the push-fit bulb holder (16) from the back of the courtesy light or clock and unscrew the bulb (17).

Cigar-lighter illumination. To change a bulb, withdraw the centre console for access. Squeeze the sides of the bulb hood (18) and remove the hood. Remove the bulb holder (19) from the hood clip and remove the bayonet fixing type bulb (20).

Seat belt and brake warning lamp. To change a bulb, withdraw the centre console for access, remove the push-fit bulb holder (21) from the lamp and remove the bayonet fixing the bulb (22).

Heater control illumination. To change a bulb, withdraw the centre console for access. Remove the push-fit bulb holder (23) from the back of the control and remove the bayonet fixing type bulb (24).

Fitting the centre console. Secure the console in position with the four screws (14). Refit the arm-rest, threading the gaiter through the hole in the arm-rest, ensuring that the screw holes of the gaiter are aligned with the holes in the arm-rest. Secure the retaining ring with the four screws (10), ensuring that the short screw is at the front. Lift the arm-rest and fit the rear securing screw (12).

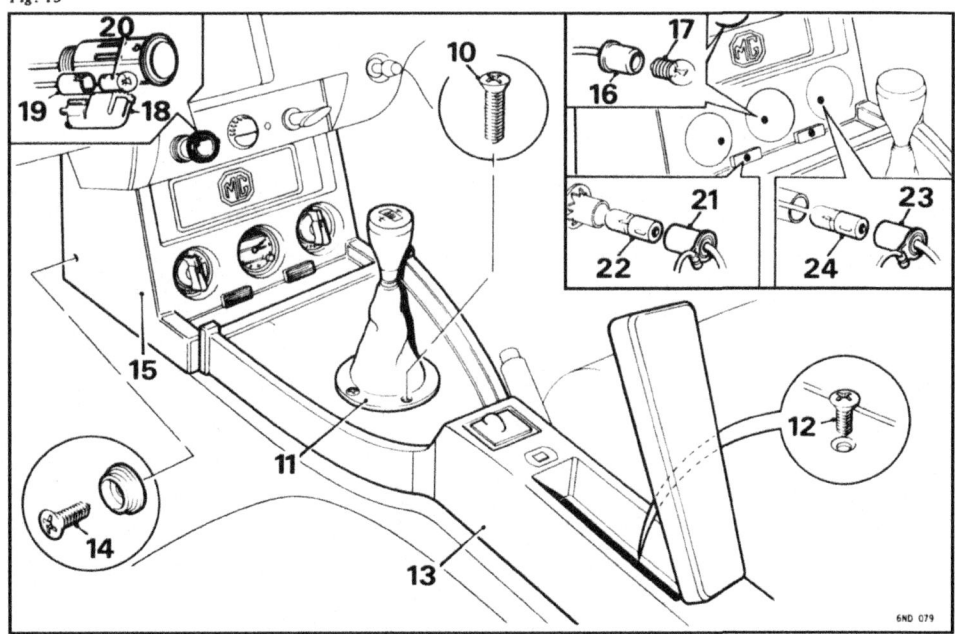

Fig. 13

Electrical

		Volts	Watts	Part No.
Replacement bulbs	Headlamp	12	60/55	GLB 472
	Pilot lamps..	12	5	GLB 223
	Stop/tail	12	5/21	GLB 380
	Reverse	12	18	BFS 273
	Number-plate lamp	12	4	BFS 233
	Direction indicator	12	21	GLB 382
	Instrument illumination	12	2·2	GLB 987
	Ignition warning	12	2	GLB 281
	Main beam..	12	2	GLB 281
	Direction indicator warning lamp	12	2	GLB 281
	Panel illumination lamp	12	2·2	GLB 987
	Cigar-lighter illlumination	12	2·2	GLB 643
	Luggage compartment lamp	12	6	GLB 254
	Courtesy lamp	12	2·2	GLB 987
	Brake warning lamp	12	2	GLB 281
	Seat belt warning lamp	12	2	GLB 281
	Switch illumination	14	0·75	GLB 284
	Heater rotary control illumination	12	2	GLB 281

WINDSCREEN WIPER

Wiper arms
Fig. 14

To re-position a wiper arm on the spindle, hold the spring clip (1) clear of the retaining groove in the spindle and withdraw the arm. Replace the arm in the required position and push it down onto the spindle (2) until it is secured in position by the retaining clip.

Wiper blade
Fig. 14

To renew a wiper blade, pull the arm away from the windscreen. Hold the fastener (3) and the spring retainer (4) away from the wiper arm (5) and withdraw the blade assembly from the arm.

Insert the end of the wiper arm into the spring fastener of the new blade and push the blade into engagement (6) with the arm.

To ensure efficient wiping it is recommended that wiper blades are renewed annually.

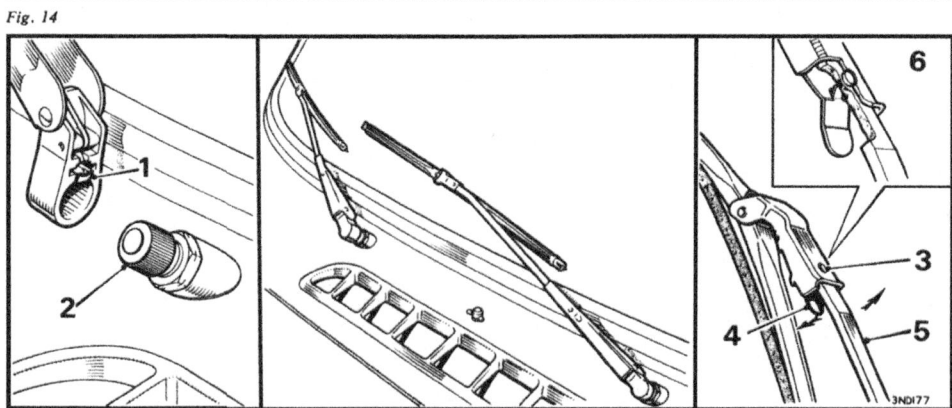

Fig. 14

Windscreen washer
Fig. 15

The windscreen washer system should be checked for correct operation and the reservoir refilled if necessary every week and before a long journey in addition to the mileage intervals given in **'MAINTENANCE SUMMARY'**.

Washer reservoir. To fill the reservoir, remove the cap (1) and lift the reservoir (2) from its mounting.

The reservoir should be filled with a mixture of water and **UNIPART Screenwash** in the recommended proportions. On no account should radiator anti-freeze or methylated spirits (denatured alcohol) be used in the windscreen washer.

In freezing conditions use **UNIPART 'Four Seasons' Screenwash.**

Jet adjusting. Turn the jet (3) using a small screwdriver to adjust the height of the spray. The spray should strike the top of the windscreen.

STARTER The starter motor is mounted on the right-hand side of the engine on the flywheel housing. It requires no lubrication.

FUEL PUMP Fuel is delivered to the carburetters by an S.U. electric fuel pump.

The pump is situated inside the luggage compartment on the right-hand side.

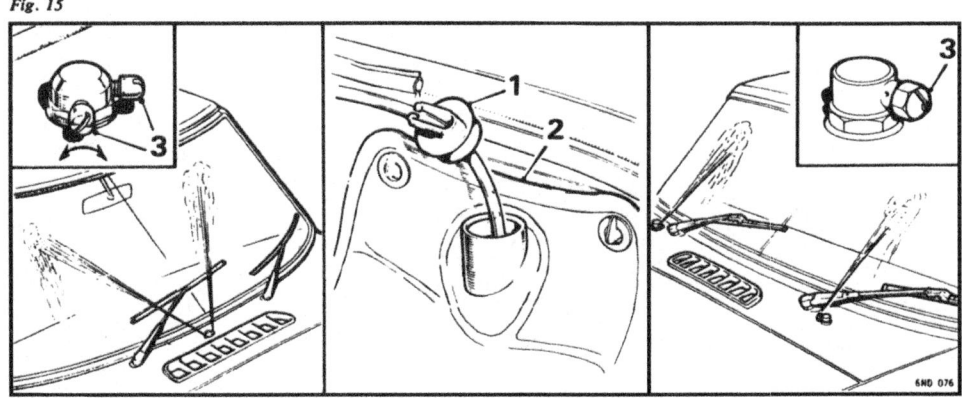

Fig. 15

IGNITION

Ignition timing — Electronic test equipment should be used to check the ignition setting (see 'GENERAL DATA') and the automatic advance. Checking and adjusting should be entrusted to your Distributor/Dealer.

Distributor
Fig. 1 — Release the retaining clips and remove the distributor cover. Remove the rotor arm (1).

Cleaning contacts. Inspect the contact points (2), and if burned, clean with fine emery cloth or a fine carborundum stone. Wipe the contacts clean with a fuel-moistened cloth. Renew the contact set if the points are pitted or worn.

Lubrication. Very lightly smear the cam (3) and pivot post (4) with grease. Add a few drops of oil to the felt pad (5) in the top of the cam spindle and through the gap (6) between the contact plate and the cam spindle to lubricate the centrifugal weights.

Do not oil the cam wiping pad.

Every 24,000 miles (40000 km), in addition to the routine maintenance, lubricate the contact breaker assembly centre bearing with a drop of oil in each of the two holes (7) in the base plate.

Carefully wipe away all surplus lubricant and see that the contact breaker points are perfectly clean and dry.

Contact gap. Turn the crankshaft until the points are fully open. Check the contact gap (2) with a feeler gauge (see 'GENERAL DATA'), the gauge should be a sliding fit. If the gap varies appreciably from the gauge thickness, slacken the contact set securing screw (8) and adjust the gap by inserting a screwdriver between the slot at the end of the plate and the pip; turn anti-clockwise (9) to increase and clockwise (10) to decrease the gap. Retighten the securing screw.

Refit the rotor arm, engage the slot in the spindle and push down firmly. Wipe the inside and outside of the distributor cover clean, particularly between the electrodes and refit the cover.

Fig. 1

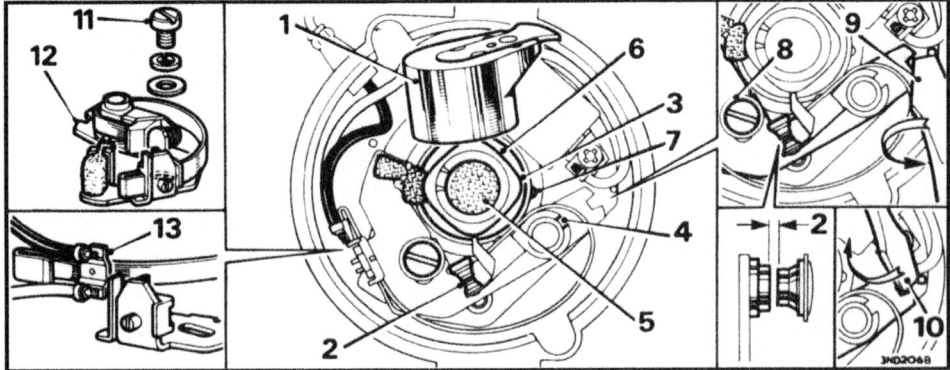

Contact set renewing. Remove the securing screw (11) with its spring and the flat washer, lift the contact set (12), press the spring and release the terminal plate (13) from the end of the spring. Before fitting the new contact set wipe the points clean with fuel or methylated spirit and very lightly grease the pivot post (4).

Re-connect the terminal plate (13) to the end of the contact breaker spring, position the contact set on the distributor base plate and lightly tighten securing screw (11). Ensure that the contact breaker spring is firmly in its register on the insulator, and set the contact gap.

Whenever a new contact set has been fitted, re-check the gap after the first 500 miles (800 km). During this period the heel of the contact will have bedded-in and reduced the gap.

Spark plugs
Fig. 2
Disconnect the H.T. lead from each plug, and partly unscrew plug. Clean the area of the cylinder head surrounding the seating of each plug, then unscrew each plug.

The spark plugs should be cleaned, preferably with an air-blast service unit.

When fitting new spark plugs ensure that only the recommended type and grade are used (see 'GENERAL DATA').

Check the plug gaps, and reset if necessary to the recommended gap (see 'GENERAL DATA'). To reset, use a special Champion spark plug gauge and setting tool; move the side electrode, never the centre one.

Screw the plug down by hand as far as possible, then use a spanner for tightening only. Always use a tubular box spanner to avoid possible damage to the insulator, and do not under any circumstances use a movable wrench. Never overtighten a plug, but ensure that a good joint is made between the plug body, washer, and cylinder head. Wipe clean the outside of the plugs before reconnecting the H.T. leads.

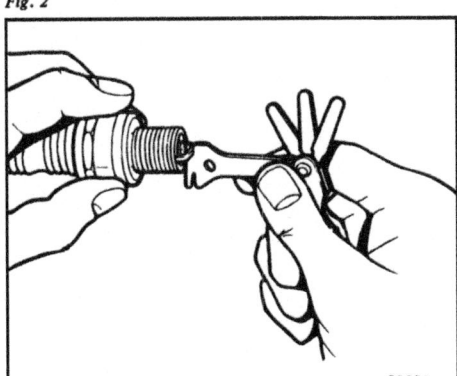

Fig. 2

ENGINE

LUBRICATION

Checking
Fig. 1
The level of the oil in the engine sump is indicated by the dipstick (1) on the right-hand side of the engine. Maintain the level between the 'MAX' and 'MIN' mark on the dipstick and never allow it to fall below the 'MIN' mark.

The filler (2) is on the forward end of the rocker cover and is provided with a quick-action cap.

Ensure that the dipstick is correctly refitted.

The oil level should always be checked before a long journey.

Draining
Fig. 1
To drain the engine oil, remove the drain plug (3) located on the right-hand side at the rear of the sump. This operation should be carried out while the engine is warm.

Clean the drain plug; check that its copper sealing washer is in a satisfactory condition, and refit.

Filling Fill the engine with the correct quantity (see **'GENERAL DATA'**) of a recommended oil. Run the engine for a short while, then allow it to stand for a few minutes before checking the level with the dipstick.

Oil filler cap
Fig. 1
An air filter is incorporated in the oil filler cap (2). The cap and filter are renewed only as a complete assembly.

Fig. 1

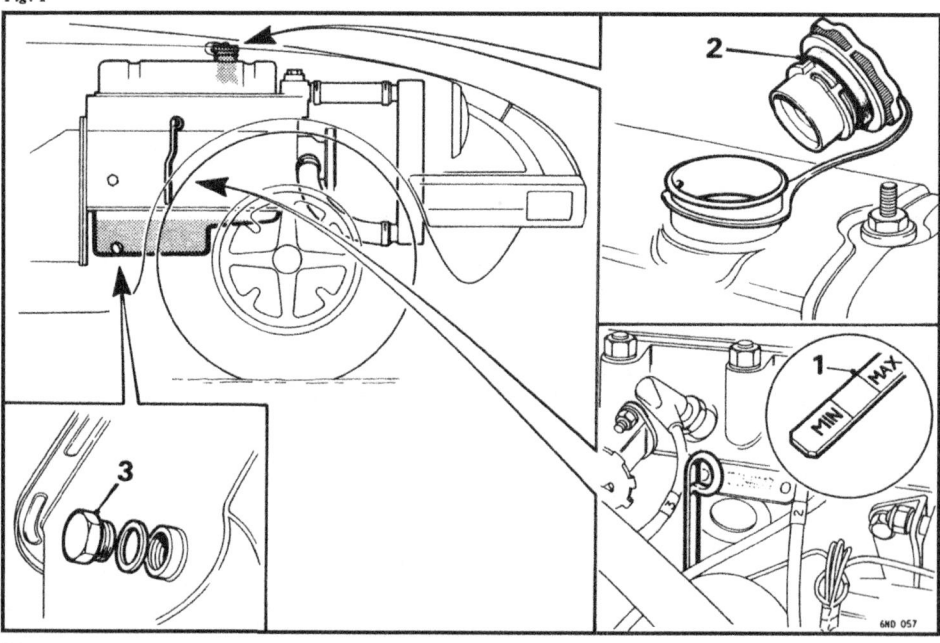

Oil filter changing
Fig. 2

The oil filter is a disposable cartridge type.

To renew, unscrew the cartridge (1) from the filter head (2) and discard the cartridge.

NOTE: If difficulty in unscrewing the cartridge is experienced, consult your Distributor or Dealer.

Smear the new seal (3) with engine oil and fit it into its groove in the new cartridge. Screw the cartridge to the filter head using hand force only.

Refill the engine with the correct quantity of a recommended lubricant, start the engine and check for oil leakage.

DRIVE BELT
Alternator
Fig. 3

Tension. When correctly tensioned, a total deflection of ½ in (13 mm) under moderate hand pressure should be possible at the midway point of the longest belt run between the pulleys.

Adjusting. To adjust the belt tension, slacken the securing bolts (1) and adjusting link nuts (2), and move the alternator to the required position. Apply any leverage necessary to the alternator end bracket (3) only and not to any other part; to avoid damaging the drive-end bracket the lever should preferably be of wood or soft metal. Tighten the bolts and re-check the belt tension. **DO NOT OVER-TIGHTEN** as this will impose an excess loading on the drive bearings.

Cleaning. Keep the slots in the plastic end-cover (4) clean.

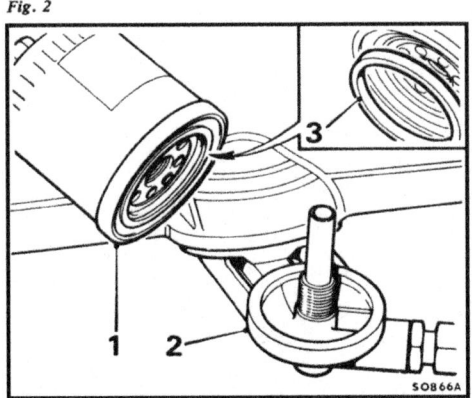

Fig. 2

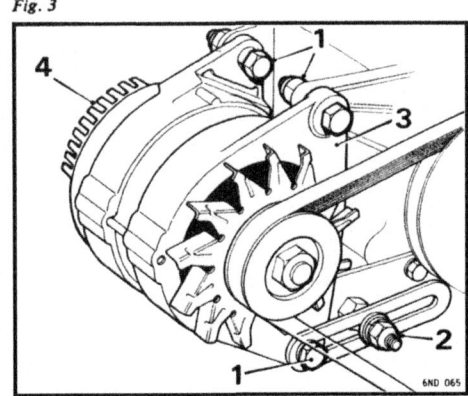

Fig. 3

Engine

VALVE ROCKER CLEARANCE

Checking Disconnect the vacuum pipe at the distributor, remove the two nuts (1) and
Fig. 4 release the heater water pipe (2) from the studs. Unscrew the two retaining nuts (3) and remove the rocker cover (4). Insert a 0·013 in (0·33 mm) feeler gauge (5) between the valve rocker arms and the valve stem. The gauge should be a sliding fit when the engine is warm. To rotate the crankshaft, engage fourth gear and pull the car forwards. Check each clearance in the following order:

Check No. 1 valve with No. 8 fully open. Check No. 8 valve with No. 1 fully open.
,, ,, 3 ,, ,, ,, 6 ,, ,, ,, ,, 6 ,, ,, ,, 3 ,, ,,
,, ,, 5 ,, ,, ,, 4 ,, ,, ,, ,, 4 ,, ,, ,, 5 ,, ,,
,, ,, 2 ,, ,, ,, 7 ,, ,, ,, ,, 7 ,, ,, ,, 2 ,, ,,

Adjusting Use a large screwdriver and ½ inch A.F. ring spanner. Slacken the locknut (6)
Fig. 4 and rotate the adjusting screw (7) clockwise to reduce or anti-clockwise to increase the clearance. Retighten the locknut, holding the screw against rotation with the screwdriver.

Refitting Check the rocker cover gasket (8) for damage; fit a new gasket if necessary.
Fig. 4 Refit the rocker cover.

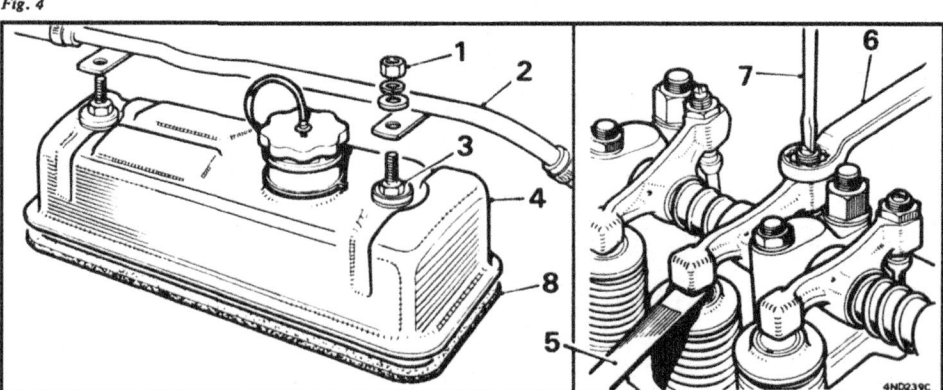

Fig. 4

FUEL SYSTEM

AIR CLEANERS
Fig. 1
The elements of both air cleaners must be renewed every 12,000 miles (20000 km) or 12 months; more frequent changes may be necessary in dusty operating conditions.

Renewing
To renew an element, unscrew the bolts (1) securing the air cleaner assembly to the carburetter and lift it from the car. Remove the base plate (2) and withdraw the element (3). Clean the inside of the casing (4) thoroughly and reassemble using a new element.

CARBURETTERS

Air pollution control
The carburetter incorporates features which assist in reducing exhaust emission. Maladjustment or the fitting of parts not to the required specification may render these features ineffective.

Carburetter damper topping-up
Fig. 2
Each damper reservoir must be topped up periodically with a recommended engine oil. **Under no circumstances should heavy-bodied lubricant be used.** Unscrew the damper cap (1), withdraw the damper, and top up the reservoir until the oil level (arrowed) is ½ in (12 mm) above the top of the hollow piston rod. Push the damper assembly back into position and screw the cap firmly into the reservoir.

Accelerator
Lubricate the carburetter accelerator and choke linkages and cables, and the accelerator pedal fulcrum.

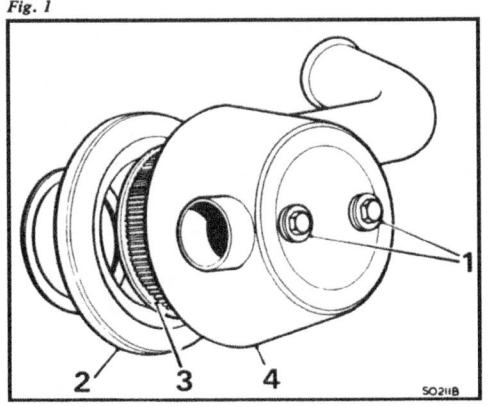
Fig. 1

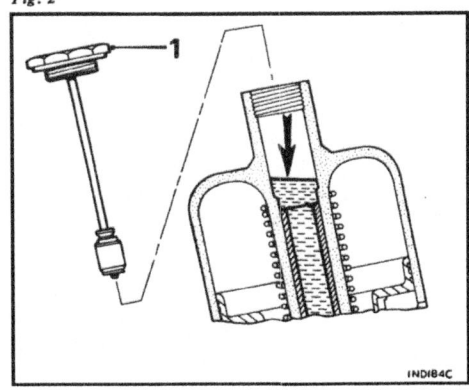
Fig. 2

Fuel System

Carburetter tuning The efficient operation of the engine and any exhaust emission control equipment which may be fitted depends not only on correct carburetter settings. It is essential that ignition timing, valve rocker clearances, distributor contact breaker and spark plug gaps are checked before setting the carburetter.

Carburetter tuning must be confined to setting the idle and fast idle speeds and the mixture at idling speed. This work should be entrusted to your Distributor or Dealer.

IMPORTANT: Where a car must conform to exhaust emission control regulations, adjustments should only be carried out if an accurate tachometer, carburetter balance meter, and exhaust gas analyser (CO meter) are available.

FUEL LINE FILTER

The filter must be renewed every 12,000 miles (20000 km) or 12 months.

Renewing the filter Remove the screw (1) securing the feed pipe and release the pipe from the clip (2) on the wing valance. Squeeze the ends of the clip and remove the fuel pump delivery hose (3) from the filter. Squeeze the ends of the clip securing the carburetter feed hose (4), remove and discard the filter (5).
Fig. 3

Fit the hoses to a new filter, ensuring that the end of the filter marked 'IN' is connected to the fuel pump delivery hose (3).

Fig. 3

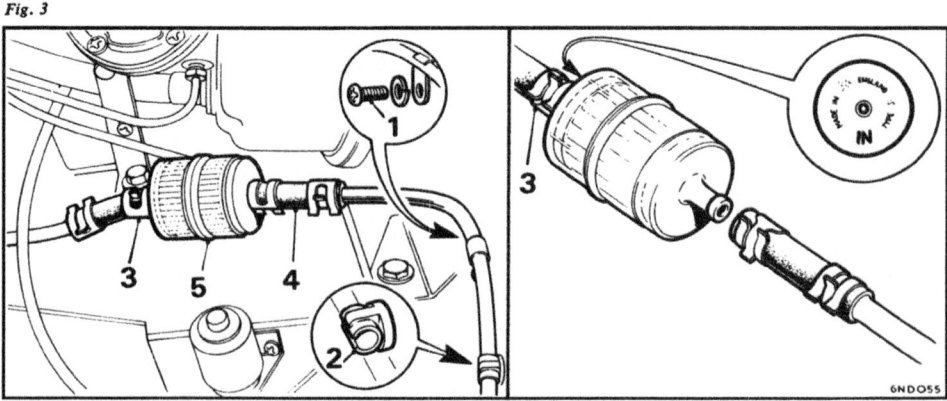

TRANSMISSION

GEARBOX *Fig. 1*
Checking From underneath the car, remove the oil level filler plug (1) and check the oil level. The correct level is at bottom of the filler level plug hole.

OVERDRIVE *Fig. 1*
Draining Remove the plug (2) to drain the oil from the gearbox and overdrive unit.

Sump filter Drain the gearbox and overdrive unit.

Clean the sump cover and its surroundings. Remove the cover securing screws, withdraw the cover (3) and the filter (4). Clean all metallic particles from the two magnets fitted to the inside of the cover, wash the cover and filter in petrol (fuel). Refit the filter and cover.

Relief valve filter Remove the plug and the seal (5); withdraw the relief valve approximately $\frac{1}{2}$ in and remove the filter (6). Wash the filter, plug and seal in petrol (fuel).

Fit the filter to the relief valve, push the valve fully home and refit the plug and seal.

Filling Fill the gearbox and overdrive unit through the oil level filler plug hole (1) with the correct quantity (see **'GENERAL DATA'**) of one of the recommended oils. Refit the plug. Run the car for a short distance, allow it to stand for a few minutes, then re-check the level. **Anti-friction additives must not be used in the gearbox or overdrive.**

Fig. 1

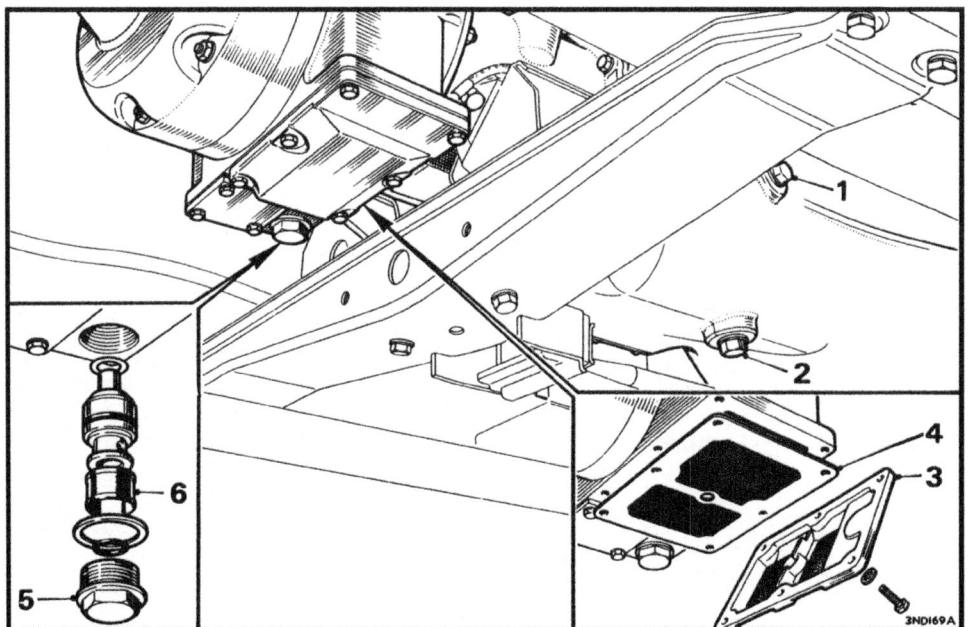

Transmission

REAR AXLE

Checking A combined oil filler and level plug (1) is located on the rear of the axle. The
Fig. 2 oil level must be maintained at the bottom of the plug aperture; ensure that the car is standing level when checking. After topping up the oil level, allow sufficient time for any surplus oil which may have been added to run out of the aperture before replacing the plug.

Do not drain the rear axle when the After-sales Service is carried out.

PROPELLER SHAFT

Lubrication A nipple (1) is provided at the front end of the propeller shaft for lubricating the
Fig. 3 sliding yoke. To lubricate, give three or four strokes of a gun filled with a recommended grease.

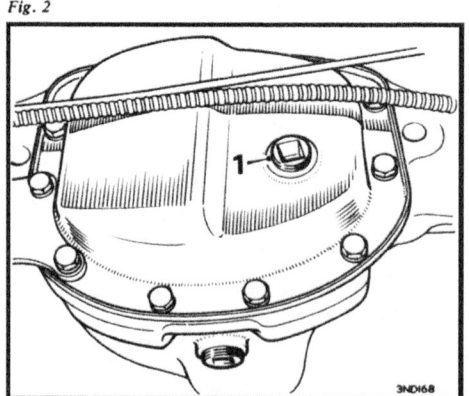

Fig. 2

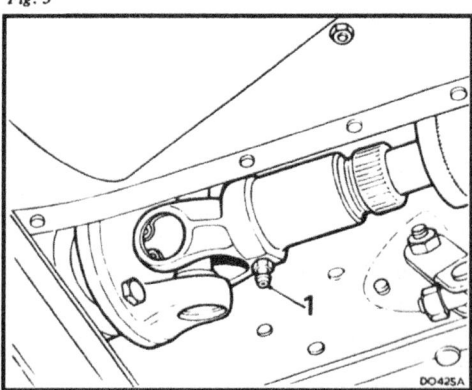

Fig. 3

STEERING/SUSPENSION

STEERING
Wheel alignment
Fig. 1

Incorrect wheel alignment can cause excessive and uneven tyre wear.

The front wheels must be set so that the distance (A) is $\frac{1}{16}$ in (1·6 mm) to $\frac{3}{32}$ in (2·4 mm) (toe in) less than the distance (B).

Wheel alignment requires the use of a special gauge and this work should be entrusted to your Distributor or Dealer.

SUSPENSION
Lubrication
Fig. 2

The three lubricating nipples (arrowed) on each of the swivel pins should be charged periodically with one of the recommended greases.

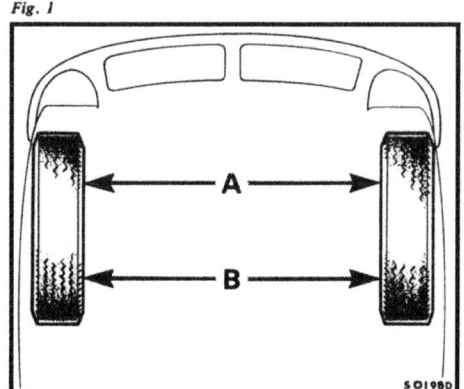
Fig. 1

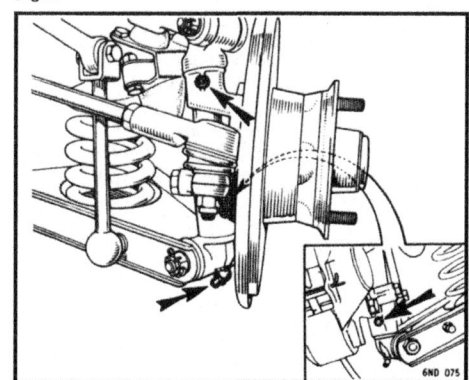
Fig. 2

GENERAL DATA

The vehicle specification may vary according to market requirements and from model to model. The manufacturers reserve the right to alter specifications with or without notice at any time. The policy of constant product improvement by the manufacturers may involve major or minor changes to the vehicle specification. Whilst every effort is made to ensure accuracy of the particulars contained in this Handbook, no liability for inaccuracies or the consequences thereof can be accepted by the manufacturer or the Dealer or Distributor who supplied the Handbook.

During running-in from new certain adjustments vary from the specification figures detailed. They will be set to specification by your Dealer or Distributor at the **After Sales Free Service** and should thereafter be maintained throughout the car's life.

Engine	Type	18V	
	Bore	3·16 in	80·3 mm
	Stroke	3·5 in	88·9 mm
	No. of cylinders	4	
	Capacity	109·8 in^3	1798 cm^3
	Compression ratio	9·0 : 1	
	Firing order	1, 3, 4, 2	
	Valve rocker clearance (set warm)	0·013 in	0·33 mm
	Oil pressure: Idling	10 to 25 lbf/in^2	0·7 to 1·7 kgf/cm^2
	Normal	50 to 80 lbf/in^2	3·5 to 5·6 kgf/cm^2
	Idle speed	750 rev/min	
	Fast idle speed	1300 rev/min	
Ignition	Stroboscopic ignition timing	10° B.T.D.C. at 1000 rev/min (vacuum advance disconnected)	
	Timing marks	Notch on crankshaft pulley, pointers on timing chain cover	
	Contact breaker gap	0·014 to 0·016 in	0·36 to 0·41 mm
	Spark plugs	Champion RN-9Y	
	Plug gap	0·035 in	0·90 mm
Fuel system	Recommended octane rating	97 and above	
	Carburetter	Two S.U. type HIF4	
	Needle	ACD	
	Spring	Red	
	Fuel pump	S.U. type AUF 305 electric	
	Exhaust gas content (carbon monoxide) at idle speed	3% CO	

Gearbox and overdrive	Overdrive ratio		0.82 : 1		
	Overall ratios: First		13.303 : 1		
	Second		8.47 : 1	*Overdrive*	
	Third		5.40 : 1	4.43 : 1	
	Fourth		3.909 : 1	3.20 : 1	
	Reverse		12.098 : 1		
	Top gear speed per 1,000 rev/min:				
	Standard		18 m.p.h. (29 km/h)		
	Overdrive		22 m.p.h. (35 km/h)		
Capacities	Fuel tank		12 gal	14.41 U.S. gal	54.54 litres
	Cooling system		11¼ pt	13.8 U.S. pt	6.6 litres
	Cooling system with heater		12 pt	14.4 U.S. pt	6.8 litres
	Engine sump		5¼ pt	6 U.S. pt	3 litres
	Engine sump with filter change		6 pt	7.25 U.S. pt	3.4 litres
	Gearbox		5 pt	6 U.S. pt	2.84 litres
	Gearbox with overdrive		6 pt	7.25 U.S. pt	3.4 litres
	Rear axle		1½ pt	2 U.S. pt	0.85 litre
Dimensions	Length		13 ft 2¼ in	4 m	
	Width		4 ft 11 15/16 in	152.3 cm	
	Height, hood erected		4 ft 2⅞ in	129.2 cm	
	Ground clearance (minimum)		4 3/16 in	106 mm	
	Track:				
	Pressed spoked wheel:				
	Front		4 ft 1½ in	124.7 cm	
	Rear		4 ft 1¾ in	126.4 cm	
	Wire wheel:				
	Front		4 ft 1 in	124.4 cm	
	Rear		4 ft 1¼ in	125 cm	
	Wheelbase		7 ft 7⅛ in	231.5 cm	
	Turning circle (kerb to kerb)		32 ft	9.75 m	
	Toe in		1/16 to 3/32 in	1.5 to 2.3 mm	
Wheels and tyres	Wheel size: Pressed spoked		5J FH × 14		
	Wire		4½J × 14 (60 spoke)		
	Tyre size/type		165SR—14 Radial-ply		

Tyre pressures

Condition	Front			Rear		
	lbf/in²	*kgf/cm²*	*bars*	*lbf/in²*	*kgf/cm²*	*bars*
Normal car weight	21	1.48	1.45	24	1.69	1.66
Gross car weight and sustained speed	21	1.48	1.45	26	1.83	1.79

It is recommended that for sustained speeds at near maximum the above tyre pressures are increased by 6 lbf/in² (0.42 kgf/cm², 0.32 bars).

Refer to page 66 for 'Weights'

General Data

Weights

	Loading condition	Total weight		Distribution			
				Front		Rear	
		Tourer	*GT*	*Tourer*	*GT*	*Tourer*	*GT*
Kerbside	Including full fuel tank and all optional extras	2,394 lb (1088 kg)	2,446 lb (1110 kg)	1,216 lb (551 kg)	1,198 lb (543 kg)	1,178 lb (534 kg)	1,248 lb (566 kg)
Normal	Kerbside weight including driver and passenger	2,694 lb (1223 kg)	2,746 lb (1245 kg)	1,332 lb (604 kg)	1,314 lb (596 kg)	1,362 lb (618 kg)	1,432 lb (649 kg)
Gross	Maximum weight condition—refer to note below	2,814 lb (1277 kg)	2,866 lb (1301 kg)	1,285 lb (583 kg)	1,267 lb (574 kg)	1,529 lb (693 kg)	1,599 lb (725 kg)
Maximum permissible towing weight		1,680 lb (762 kg)	1,680 lb (762 kg)				
Maximum towbar hitch load		100 lb (45 kg)	100 lb (45 kg)				
Maximum roof rack load			50 lb (23 kg)				

NOTE: Due consideration must be given to the overall weight carried when fully loading the car. Any load carried on a luggage rack (Tourer) or roof rack (GT) or downward load from a towing hitch must also be included in the maximum loading.

LEYLAND ST

Leyland ST market a wide range of specialized parts and accessories to increase the performance of your car, both for competition work and road use. Various stages of engine tune can be obtained by fitting the appropriate Pluspac. Each Pluspac is a complete kit, and contains detailed fitting instructions.

Leyland ST Plusparts are also available to up-rate other systems of the car, such as brakes and suspension, in line with the increased engine performance.

Your new car in its standard form is designed and tuned to give maximum performance consistent with the highest degree of reliability. Tuning above the standard level will tend to reduce this reliability and consequently the fitting of Pluspacs, other than Pluspac 'A', could invalidate the Owners Service Statement. However, reliability will be at least comparable with other cars giving similar performance.

In certain countries legislation exists covering air pollution, safety or noise limitations on motor vehicles. Before a car is super-tuned or modified, it is the responsibility of the owner to ensure that the proposed alterations and additions are either approved by the appropriate authority for use on the road, or do not contravene the standards set by legislation.

Leyland ST Parts can be obtained from Leyland ST Distributors and Stockists throughout the U.K. A complete list of Distributors and Stockists, together with information on Pluspacs or Plusparts available for your car can be obtained from:

Leyland ST
Abingdon-on Thames, Oxfordshire OX14 1AU
Telephone: 0235 25251

SNA 004 B

MAINTENANCE SUMMARY

LEYCARE SERVICE

British Leyland Distributors and Dealers operating Leycare Service will, on request, provide a copy of the Leycare Service Job Sheet giving exact details of the work carried out at the prescribed interval and of any further work required. Leycare Service Job Sheets are updated as modifications affecting routine maintenance are introduced and as a result may differ from the Maintenance Summary content published in this Handbook.

Detailed maintenance instructions will be found on the page in brackets after each item.

In addition to the periodic maintenance the following checks should be made weekly:
Check/top up engine oil (56)
Check/top up brake fluid reservoir (41)
Check/top up battery electrolyte (43)
Check/top up cooling system (33)
Check/top up washer reservoir (53)
Check function of original equipment, i.e. exterior lamps, wipers, and warning indicators
Check tyres for tread depth, visually for external cuts in fabric, exposure of ply or cord structure, lumps and bulges.
Check/adjust tyre pressures, including spare (37, 65)
Check tightness of wheel fastenings (36)

MAINTENANCE INTERVALS

Carry out the services indicated by **X** in column

A at 6,000-mile (10000-km) or 6-month intervals
B at 12,000-mile (20000-km) or 12-month intervals

Items included in the 3,000-mile (5000-km) or 3-month interval Inspection Check are indicated in **column C**

	A	B	C
ENGINE			
Check/top up engine oil (56)			X
Renew engine oil and filter (57)	X	X	
Renew carburetter air cleaner elements (59)		X	
Top up carburetter piston dampers (59)	X	X	
Check/adjust carburetter idle speed and mixture settings*	X	X	
Renew fuel filter (60)		X	
Renew engine filler cap (56)		X	
Check/adjust valve clearances (58)		X	
Check cooling/heater systems for leaks and hoses for security and condition	X	X	X
Check/top up cooling system (33)	X	X	X
Check/adjust operation of screen washers and top up reservoir (53)	X	X	X
Check driving belt; adjust or renew (57)	X	X	X
Lubricate accelerator control linkage (and pedal pivot)—check operation (76)	X	X	

68

	A	B	C
IGNITION			
Clean/adjust spark plugs (55)	X		
Renew spark plugs (55)		X	
Check distributor points; adjust or renew (54)	X	X	
Lubricate distributor (54)	X	X	
Check/adjust ignition timing and distributor characteristics using electronic equipment*	X	X	
TRANSMISSION			
Check/top up gearbox and rear axle oil (61 and 62)	X	X	
Check/top up clutch fluid reservoir (41)	X	X	X
Lubricate propeller shaft (62)	X	X	
Gearbox with overdrive—drain, clean filters, and fill with new oil (61)	Every 24,000 miles (40000 km) or 24 months		
STEERING AND SUSPENSION			
Check steering rack for oil leaks	X	X	X
Check hydraulic dampers for fluid leaks	X	X	X
Check condition and security of steering unit joints and gaiter	X	X	X
Check/adjust front wheel alignment*	X	X	
Lubricate all grease points, excluding hubs (63)	X	X	
BRAKES			
Check visually hydraulic pipes and unions for chafing, leaks and corrosion	X	X	X
Check/top up brake fluid reservoir (41)	X	X	X
Check/adjust foot brake and hand brake operation (39)	X	X	X
Inspect brake pads for wear, discs for condition (39)	X		
Inspect brake linings/pads for wear, drums/discs for condition (39 and 40)		X	
Lubricate hand brake mechanical linkage (and cables) (39)	X	X	
Clean servo filter element (41)		X	
ELECTRICAL			
Check function of original equipment, i.e. interior and exterior lamps, screen wipers, horns, and warning indicators	X	X	X
Check/top up battery electrolyte (43)	X	X	X
Clean and grease battery connections	X	X	
Check/adjust headlamp alignment*	X	X	X
Check, if necessary renew, windscreen wiper blades (52)	X	X	X
EXHAUST, FUEL AND CLUTCH PIPES			
Check clutch pipes for leaks and chafing	X	X	X
Check fuel system for leaks, pipes and unions for chafing and corrosion*	X	X	X
Check exhaust system for leaks and security	X	X	X
Check fuel filler tank connections	X	X	X

Maintenance Summary

	A	B	C
WHEELS AND TYRES			
Check that tyres comply with manufacturer's specification (65)	x	x	x
Check/adjust tyre pressures including spare (37, 65)	x	x	x
Check tyres for tread depth, visually for cuts in fabric, exposure of ply or cord structure, lumps or bulges	x	x	x
Check tightness of road wheel fastenings (36)	x	x	x
BODY			
Lubricate all locks and hinges (**not steering lock**)	x	x	
Check condition and security of seats and seat belts	x	x	x
Check rear view mirrors for cracks and crazing	x	x	x
GENERAL			
Road/roller test and check function of all instrumentation*	x	x	
Report any additional work required*			

* Your Distributor or Dealer should check these items

NOTE: Take the advice of your Distributor or Dealer on the need for:
1. More frequent engine oil changes;
2. Additional brake maintenance (42)

NOTES

SERVICE

Identification When communicating with your Distributor or Dealer always quote the car and
Fig. 1 engine numbers. When the communication concerns the transmission units or body
details it is necessary to quote also the transmission casing and body numbers.

(1) **Car number.** Stamped on a plate secured to the right-hand valance.

(2) **Engine number.** Stamped on a plate secured to the right-hand side of the cylinder block, or stamped directly onto the cylinder block.

(3) **Gearbox number.** Stamped on the right-hand side of the gearbox casing.

(4) **Overdrive unit number.** Stamped on a plate secured to the underside of the overdrive main casing.

(5) **Rear axle number.** Stamped on the left-hand side of the rear axle tube near the spring seating.

Fig. 1

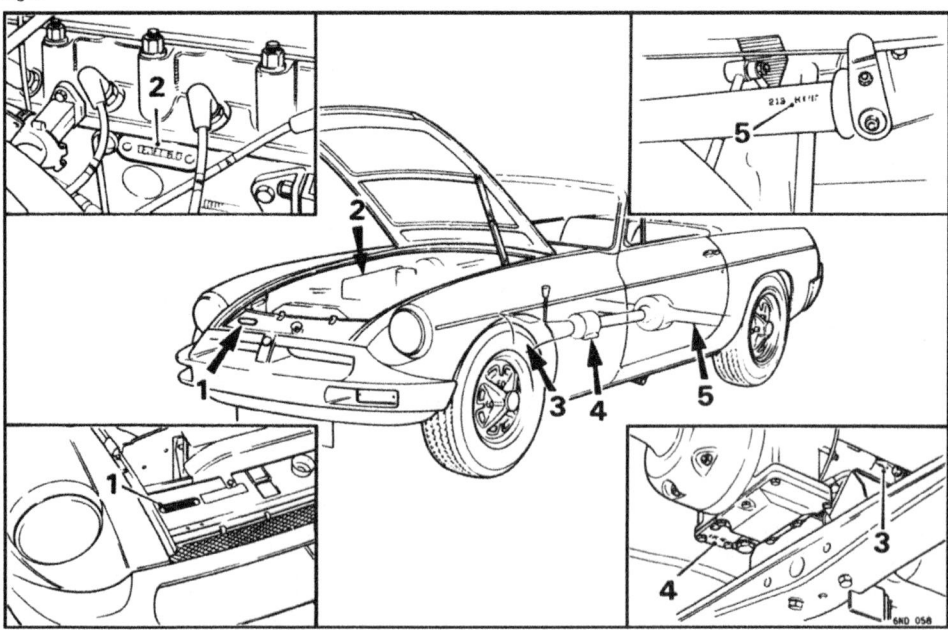

Service

Service Your **Distributor or Dealer** is provided with the latest information concerning special service tools and workshop techniques. This enables him to undertake your service and repairs in the most efficient and economic manner.

The **Passport to Service** supplied with your vehicle includes provision for recording regular maintenance service. It is in your interest to use this facility and to ensure that the servicing Distributor or Dealer stamps the Passport against the appropriate service. Regular maintenance is the best safeguard against the possibility of abnormal repair bills at a later date. Failure to have your car correctly maintained could invalidate the terms defined in the Owners Service Statement.

A Passport to Service with a completed maintenance record is proof of regular servicing and could well enhance the value of your vehicle in the eyes of a prospective buyer. A replacement **Passport to Service** is obtainable from **Distributors or Dealers**.

By keeping the Passport to Service, signed by the Distributor, Dealer or vendor, in the vehicle, you can quickly establish the date of purchase and provide the necessary details if adjustments are required to be carried out under the terms of the Owners Service Statement.

Claims for the replacement of parts under the terms of the Owners Service Statement must be submitted to the supplying Distributor or Dealer, or when this is not possible, to the nearest Distributor or Dealer, informing them of the vendor's name and address. Except in emergency, work carried out under the terms of the Owners Service Statement should always be carried out by an appointed Distributor or Dealer.

Service parts and accessories Genuine BRITISH LEYLAND and UNIPART parts and accessories are designed and tested for your vehicle and have the full backing of the Leyland Owners Service Statement. ONLY WHEN GENUINE LEYLAND AND UNIPART PARTS ARE USED CAN RESPONSIBILITY BE CONSIDERED UNDER THE TERMS OF THE STATEMENT.

In accordance with the Company's policy of continuing improvement, new items are introduced regularly into the **UNIPART** range. **UNIPART** parts should be used when servicing or replacing parts on your car.

For more information on **UNIPART**, see your Leyland Distributor or Dealer.

Genuine British Leyland and UNIPART parts and accessories are supplied in cartons and packs bearing either or both of these symbols.

Safety features embodied in the car may be impaired if other than genuine parts are fitted. In certain territories, legislation prohibits the fitting of parts not to the vehicle manufacturer's specification. Owners purchasing accessories while travelling abroad should ensure that the accessory and its fitted location on the car conform to mandatory requirements existing in their country of origin.

Service Exchange Scheme The Service Exchange Scheme has been designed as a money-saver.

Your Distributor or Dealer will supply any exchange assembly offered for your vehicle at a price which allows for the return of the old one to us for rebuilding to 'as new' standard, at one of our specialist factories or by the original supplier.

The use of this technique reduces the cost but not the quality, and each replacement assembly carries the same warranty as a new one.

Ask your Distributor or Dealer for full details and for examples of the money you can save by taking advantage of the Service Exchange Scheme.

Supplementary tool kit A **UNIPART** Tool Kit is obtainable from all Distributors and Dealers. The kit, in a waterproof roll, contains the following tools:

8 combination spanners   2 screwdrivers
1 adjustable spanner   1 feeler gauge set
2 pairs pliers

This kit can be supplemented from a comprehensive range of **UNIPART** quality hand tools which are also available.

UNIPART car care Use of the following products selected from the **UNIPART** range will ensure maximum effectiveness in maintaining the appearance and condition of your car.

Engine grime and grease	UNIPART Engine Cleaner
Carpets }	
Seats and trim }	UNIPART Upholstery Cleaner
Headlining }	
Washing	UNIPART Car Shampoo
	UNIPART Car Sponges
	UNIPART Chamois-leather
Glass	UNIPART Glass Cleaner
Bodywork	UNIPART Hi-shine Car Polish
Chrome and bright trim	UNIPART Chrome Cleaner
Winter aids:	
Iced-up windscreen and windows	UNIPART De-icer Spray
Washer reservoir	UNIPART 'Four Seasons' Screenwash

LUBRICATION

The lubrication systems of your new car are filled with high quality oils. You should always use a high quality oil of the correct viscosity range in the engine, gearbox and rear axle during subsequent maintenance operations or when topping up. The use of oils not to the correct specification can lead to high oil and fuel consumption and ultimately do damage to the engine, gearbox or rear axle components.

Oils to the correct specification contain additives which disperse the corrosive acids formed by combustion and also prevent the formation of sludge which can block oilways. **Additional oil additives should not be used.** Servicing intervals must be adhered to.

Engine   Use a well known brand of oil to B.L.S. OL.02 or MIL-L-2104B or A.P.I, SE quality, with a viscosity band spanning the temperature range of your locality.

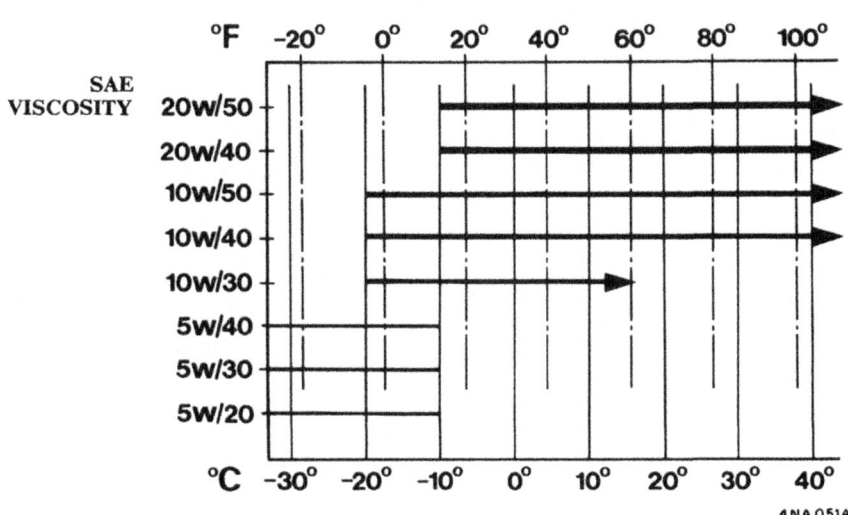

Synchromesh gearbox   Use the same oil selected for the engine.

Rear axle and steering rack   Top up and refill with H.D. 90 (MIL-L-2105B) above −10°C (10°F) or H.D. 80 (MIL-L-2105B) below −5°C (20°F).

Grease points   Use Multipurpose Lithium Grease N.L.G.I, consistency No. 2.

Lubrication

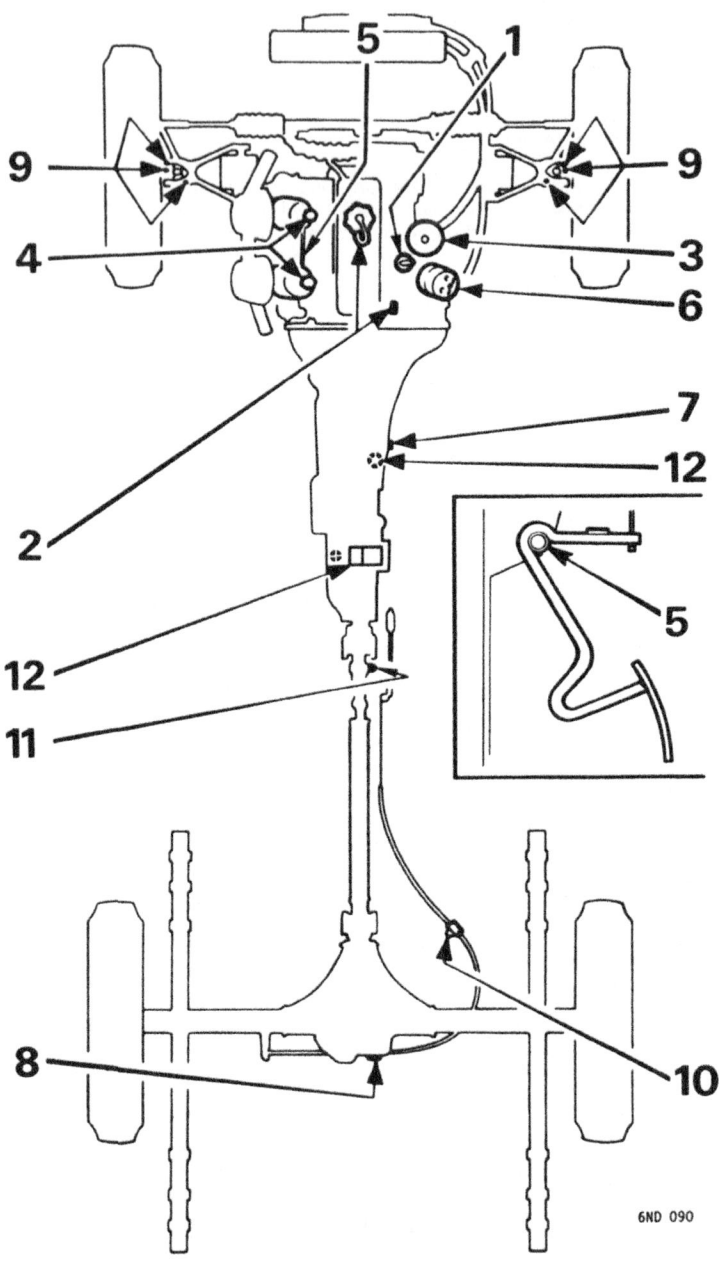

NOTE: Ensure that the car is standing on a level surface when checking the oil levels.

Weekly
(1) ENGINE. Check the oil level with the dipstick, and top up if necessary.

After switching off the engine always allow a short period of time to elapse before checking the engine oil level.

Every 3,000 miles (5000 km) or 3 months Optional Lubrication
(1) ENGINE. Check the oil level with the dipstick, and top up if necessary.

Every 6,000 miles (10000 km) or 6 months
(2) ENGINE. Drain and refill with new oil.

(3) ENGINE OIL FILTER. Remove the disposable cartridge, fit new.

(4) CARBURETTERS. Top up the carburetter piston dampers.

(5) ACCELERATOR. Lubricate accelerator control linkage, cable and pedal fulcrum.

(6) DISTRIBUTOR. Lubricate all parts as necessary.
Do not oil the cam wiping pad.

(7) GEARBOX AND OVERDRIVE. Check oil level, and top up if necessary.

(8) REAR AXLE. Check oil level, and top up if necessary.

(9) FRONT SUSPENSION (6 nipples)

(10) HAND BRAKE CABLE (1 nipple) AND MECHANICAL LINKAGE

(11) PROPELLER SHAFT (1 nipple)

Give three or four strokes with a grease gun.

LOCKS AND HINGES. Lubricate the bonnet release safety catch and all locks and hinges.
Do not oil the steering lock.

Every 24,000 miles (40000 km.) or 24 months
(12) GEARBOX WITH OVERDRIVE. Drain, clean overdrive filters and refill with new oil—ref. page 61.

Service oils and greases are given on page 78

Lubrication

SERVICE LUBRICANTS

Component	Engine, Synchromesh Gearbox and Carburetter			Rear Axle and Steering Gear		Grease Points	Upper Cylinder Lubrication
Climatic conditions	All temperatures above −10°C (15°F)	Temperatures 10° to −20°C (50° to −5°F)	All temperatures below −10°C (15°F)	All temperatures above −10°C (15°F)	All temperatures below −10°C (15°F)	All conditions	All conditions
Minimum performance level	British Leyland Service Fill Lubricating Oil Specification for Passenger Car and Light Commercial Petrol engines B.L.S. OL.02			MIL-L-2105B	MIL-L-2105B		
ESSO	Esso Uniflo 10W/50	Esso Uniflo 10W/50	Esso Extra Motor Oil 5W/20	Gear Oil GX 90/140	Esso Gear Oil GX 80	Esso Multi-purpose Grease H	Esso Upper Cylinder Lubricant
MOBIL	Mobiloil Special 20W/50 or Super 10W/50	Mobiloil Super 10W/50	Mobiloil 5W/20	Mobilube HD 90	Mobilube HD 80	Mobilgrease MP or MS	Mobil Upperlube
BP	BP Super Visco-Static 20/50 or 10W/40	BP Super Visco-Static 10W/30 or 10W/40	BP Super Visco-Static BP Super Visco-Static 5W/20	BP Hypogear 90 EP	BP Hypogear 80 EP	BP Energrease L 2	BP Upper Cylinder Lubricant
SHELL	Shell Super 20W/50	Shell Super 10W/50	Shell Super 5W/30	Shell Spirax Heavy Duty 90	Shell Spirax Heavy Duty 80	Shell Retinax A	Shell Upper Cylinder Lubricant
DUCKHAMS	Duckhams Q Motor Oil		Duckhams Q 5-30	Duckhams Hypoid 90S	Duckhams Hypoid 80S	Duckhams LB 10 Grease	Duckhams Adcoid Liquid
TEXACO	Havoline 20W/50 or 10W/40	Havoline 10W/40	Havoline 5W/30	Multigear Lubricant EP 90	Multigear Lubricant EP 80	Marfak All Purpose	Special Upper Cylinder Lubricant
PETROFINA	Fina Supergrade 20W/50 or 10W/40	Fina Supergrade 10W/50 or 10W/40	Fina Supergrade 5W/20	Fina Pentonic XP 90-140	Fina Pentonic MP 80	Fina HLT 2	Fina Cyltonic
CASTROL	CRI 5W/20	Castrolite	Castrol GTZ	Castrol Hypoy B 90	Castrol Hypoy B 80	Castrol LM Grease	Castrollo

© Copyright British Leyland Motors Corporation 1976
and Brooklands Books Limited 1992, 2009 and 2021

This book is published by Brooklands Books Limited and based upon text
and illustrations protected by copyright and first published in 1976 by
British Leyland Motors Corporation and may not be
reproduced transmitted or copied by any means without the
prior written permission of Rover Group Limited and
Brooklands Books Limited.

Brooklands Books Ltd., PO Box 904,
Amersham, HP6 9JA, England
www.brooklands-books.com

Part Number: AKM 3661

ISBN 9781869826703   Ref: MG77HH   7W4/3054